MILLION DOLLAR SPEAKER

Powerful Storytelling Frameworks to Grow Your Influence and Create Wealth from Speaking

EILEEN WILDER & JOSEPH AARON

MILLION DOLLAR SPEAKER

Powerful Storytelling Frameworks to Grow Your Influence and Create Wealth from Speaking

Copyright © 2022. Eileen Wilder and Joseph Aaron. All rights reserved. No part of this publication may be reproduced, distributed, or transmitted in any form or by any means, including photocopying, recording, or other electronic or mechanical methods, without the prior written permission of the publisher, except in the case of brief quotations embodied in critical reviews and certain other noncommercial uses permitted by copyright law. For permission requests, speaking inquiries, and bulk order purchase options, email hello@theelitespeakers.com.

Elite Speakers
1305 W 11th St. #3072
Houston, TX 77008
theelitespeakers.com

Cover and Interior Design by Transcendent Publishing
www.transcendentpublishing.com
Edited by DragonflyWings.Ink, a division of Lori Lynn Enterprises
Graphics by Tuba Shahbaz
Cover Photo by Samantha Everhart of Everhart Photography

ISBN: 978-0-9963573-2-6

Printed in the United States of America.

Oratory is the masterful art. Poetry, painting, music, sculpture, architecture please, thrill, inspire—but oratory rules.

The orator dominates those who hear him, convinces their reason, controls their judgment, compels their action. For the time being, he is master.

—David Josiah Brewer

According to most studies, people's number one fear is public speaking. Number two is death. Death is number two. Does that sound right? This means to the average person, if you go to a funeral, you're better off in the casket than doing the eulogy.

—Jerry Seinfield

CONTENTS

Advance Praise ix
Foreword xvii

Section I: Start Here 1
  1. Can I Get an AMEN? 3
  2. Your Stage Awaits — from Eileen 7
  3. What's Possible Seemed Impossible 17
  4. Who This Book Is For (and Where to Begin) 21
  5. Why Not Set an Absurd Goal? 27
  6. The Master Key to Getting Anyone to Do Anything ... 31
  7. What Is the Belief and Identity Transformation System? 37

Section II: The System 41
  8. Find Out What's Holding Your Audience Back — from Eileen 43
  9. The Power of Polarity 49
  10. Transformation Secrets of the World's Greatest Speakers: Epiphanies, Identities, and Declarations, *Oh, My!* 59
  11. Discover the Hidden Framework Used by the World's Most Persuasive Speakers — from Eileen 73
  12. Presenting with Power: How to Use Speaker Bits to Make a Point, Attack a False Belief, and Shift Thinking 81

13. Take Your Speaker Bit Techniques to the Next Level 103
14. Don't Harm Your Audience, Lead Them 119
15. Positioning Yourself to Make an Invitation Without Sounding Salesy — from Eileen 127
16. The Heaven and Hell of Creating Desire 137
17. The Three Presentation Frameworks for Your Irresistible Invitations 143
18. The New World of 6- and 7-Figure Days — from Eileen 155

Section III: Closing Words 163
19. Putting It All Together: How Million Dollar Speakers Move Their Audiences to Say Yes 165
20. You Need a "Face-Smooshing" Day of Decision 169

Speak to Us 175
Acknowledgments 177
About the Authors 181
Where to Get Your Bonuses 185

DEDICATION

To Calvin Jean, a preacher who demonstrated the power of a stage to change a young man's life. To Dr. David Norris, a mentor who taught me the power of a story. To Eric Stone, a preacher who showed me the power of connecting from stage. To Dr. Myron Golden and Russell Brunson, entrepreneurs who taught me to sell from stage.

My life and the experiences of my audiences are better as a result of your commitment to excellence in speaking. Thank you for your example. I pray my words impact my audiences' lives as yours have so deeply impacted mine.

—Joseph Aaron

To Harrison, my loving husband, who has always been willing to risk it all for the dream of making a difference and leaving a life of legacy, and for being a leader that I, our children, and so many people look up to and aspire to be like.

You rise early. You seek Wisdom. You labor long and hard. All from a place of rest. Every room you walk into becomes peace, every conversation you enter becomes grace, every deed carried out with generosity. It is both refreshing and energizing always in your presence. I am so blessed to be your wife.

—Eileen Wilder

ADVANCE PRAISE

When Joe and I did a live virtual event, I hit a new personal record: I hit a million dollars in a single day. I would never have brought in as much revenue if I didn't partner with Joe. He helped me to run the event smoothly, get the right people on, and close a ton of sales.

—**Dan Henry**, co-founder of CloseDeals.com, founder of GetClients.com, *Wall Street Journal* bestselling author of *Digital Millionaire Secrets*

The results from my event have been amazing. I went from a less than 2% conversion rate to converting at 20% and I've never done that my whole life, like ever, ever, ever! SO excited! Joe and Eileen are the best.

—**Annie Grace**, bestselling author of *This Naked Mind: Control Alcohol, Find Freedom, Discover Happiness, and Change Your Life*

What's crazy is that our speaking events literally became a movement. Because we interact so much, I'm able to connect with my students more, and that has helped us increase the quality of the programs we offer. Of course, the cash is a big bonus! I cannot thank you enough, Eileen and Joe, both of you, for helping me become the kind of person who makes a million dollars per month.

—**Kiana Danial**, CEO at Invest Diva, *USA Today* & *Wall Street Journal* bestselling author of *Million Dollar Family Secrets*

Holy. Moly. Donut. Shop. Joseph Aaron Giglietti and Eileen Wilder's training on speaking just changed the game forever!!! I love their method!! We had 2,900 registrations, 710-720 on live... 100% retention for 4.5 hours. People were raving, referring, and staying!! The framework you guys have developed is life-changing. Eileen and Joe, you're geniuses, thank you!!!

—**Rachel Pedersen,** "The Queen of Social Media," founder & CEO of award-winning social media marketing agency The Viral Touch, author of *Unfiltered: Proven Strategies to Start and Grow Your Business by Not Following the Rules*

I've tried just about every lead and customer acquisition method that you can do, but what Joe and Eileen teach was the missing link for my business. The event model and the structures they teach are unique and powerful.

—**James Hodges,** founder and CEO of REI Game Changers

As someone who has made his living running the Webinar Agency, I've generated over $100M with live events and presentations. I worked with Joe on a recent live event to specifically learn how to lead and inspire my audience, which differs from my analytical approach. The result? We had near 100% show rate and near 100% retention rate on the event, making it our most successful live event ever. And we did it all without slides. There's an art to running inspirational live events, and there's no one better than Joe at teaching and executing this model.

—**Joel Erway,** host of *Sold With Webinars* and *Experts Unleashed* podcasts, author of *High Ticket Courses*

ADVANCE PRAISE

There is so much more to public speaking than just giving your presentation. You need to engage your audience, and draw them in with rich storytelling to the point that they are literally sitting on the edge of their seats. Eileen Wilder is one of the best speakers I've seen—and this book gives you the tools you need to craft and deliver your own powerful messaging.

—**Alison J. Prince,** host of *How to Sell Online* podcast, business coach and entrepreneur, founder of four multi-million dollar brands

What Joe and Elieen understand about speaking will blow away even the most advanced speakers! I have done hundreds of presentations, and after just ONE time through their frameworks, I DOUBLED my highest close rate ever. They have figured out a way to explain and teach the most advanced techniques in a way that is simple. If you claim to be a speaker, you must understand what they teach, or I guarantee you're behind.

—**Josh Forti,** founder of 6-Figure Paydays and joshforti.com

I learned a long time ago that you can't be your best self by yourself, and I'm so grateful to have Joe and Eileen as coaches who have helped me not only become my best self but also do my best work. As a result of their guidance, my influence, my impact, and my income has increased exponentially, and I believe this book will do the same for you.

—**Dharius Daniels,** lead pastor of Change Church, author of *Relational Intelligence: The People Skills You Need for the Life of Purpose You Want*

When I first started doing virtual events, my thoughts and concerns were that I wouldn't be good enough to get people to want to first listen to me. And then secondly, I thought that I wasn't going to be good enough to get people to work with me. My experience working with Joe and Eileen has been amazing. For myself, I've been able to have a $90,000 day through an event, and just last week, I did a $30,000 day. So it's been absolutely outstanding.

—**Rowell Ramos,** host of *Wealth Creators* podcast

Joe and Eileen have totally changed how we operate our business. Before we understood the power of virtual events, we were doing webinars. But after implementing everything that Joe and Eileen taught us, we now generate in one day what we used to make in a month (and sometimes two months, and sometimes even multiple months!) It's totally changed our businesses and our lives. At the end of the day, it gave us back our most precious gift, which is time. And we can now use that time to sow into the clients that we work with. We're now actually able to serve our clients at a higher level.

—**Ryan & Lydia Ebling**, owners of Complete Body Labs

I used to struggle with believing that people would buy what I had to offer. Sometimes you're standing just in front of success, but you can't see it. Joe and Eileen helped me tweak how I was presenting my offer and how people could apply to work with me, and we have now crossed $1 million from speaking and events.

—**Rasmus Lingren**, CEO of Infospray Media

ADVANCE PRAISE

It starts with a commitment to say, "I will do this. There is nothing stopping me from being a Million Dollar Speaker. I'm going to make it happen, come hell or high water." If you have that attitude, there's no doubt in my mind that anybody who takes what Joe and Eileen teach has the ability to accomplish that. *No* doubt.

—**Marvin Mitchell**, President of Path to Prosperity

Joe & Eileen show you how to captivate your audience and take them on a mesmerizing journey, using speaking strategies like nothing I've ever seen. You'll learn to leverage the transformative power of your voice and your story and I guarantee you'll never be the same!

—**Seyi Makinde**, founder of The Brand Powerhouse

I love most, how Joe & Eileen show a true genuine passion and eagerness to impart their knowledge to their students/mentees. Even on the spot as they are learning they are teaching. I love the in-the-moment, NO-EGO transparency that we get in our trainings. I love that they wholeheartedly believe in what you do and in us as their students! I've broken through many layers and years of confusion and overthinking. I've learned to stop over complicating things. Run your ONE PLAY, over and over! Keep it simple, keep it moving. Elite Speakers CREATE DESIRE, invigorate their audiences and leave them begging for more.

—**Cherise B**, student of Six Figure Speaker

Joe and Eileen instill *confidence*. And when you use the frameworks, you will lovingly affect and change the hearts and minds of your audience—never to be the same again. Thus, you change the world. It's what words can do!

—**Tracy Keating Gunn**, The Candy Lady at Life is Sweet, founder of Get Exitable and The EASY Method

When we first had the honor of meeting Eileen and Joe at Funnel Hacking Live, we asked them what it is exactly that they do. They said the line that changed the game for us in our business forever: "We help entrepreneurs do 6- and 7-figure DAYS through virtual events." That's when our world flipped upside down and our paradigms around money were shattered forever. We immediately decided to link arms and go to work! At our first virtual event, we did $75K in revenue. These guys are rock stars!!!

—**Nick Santonastasso & Ratmir Rafikov**, Victorious International LLC

Speaking is the art of communication. To become great, you must study with the masters. Joe and Eileen will teach you the frameworks that allow you to speak in a way that transforms the belief of your audience, to help them become the ideal client, who is desperate to buy your offers. When your story becomes their story, your beliefs become their own. Study the masters to master the craft.

—**Chad Nedland**, author of *The Book on Being Better*, creator of the Story Assimilation Framework

ADVANCE PRAISE

Eileen Wilder is one of the sweetest and humblest people I know, but here's what she doesn't tell you: She hit the 2 Comma Club award in record time. She hits 7-figure days with ease. And she still keeps the focus on impact & FUN!

She understands that the biggest changes in your life actually begin with a small, quietly whispered "Yes." The tiniest surrender to possibility opens the door to explosive growth on a level you can't even see yet.

When your ROI is both impact and income, and integrity and enjoying life along the way is non-negotiable, you get to ask: "How big of an impact can we make and how much fun can we have while we make it?" It's an intoxicating question, but you only get to find out after you take action with the first small, "Yes." *YES, I'll read this book. YES, I'll go ALL-IN on myself. YES, I'll do what it takes to become a Million Dollar Speaker.*

—Jackie Lacroix, bestselling author of The Bombshell Manifesto, founder of The Bombshell Alliance

Every once in a while, you get to work with someone who not only "gets it," but GETS IT at such a high level they make everything look (and feel) easy. Joe and Eileen have created a level of mastery that is hard to find and even harder to access. The fact that they've put their best recipes in a BOOK for such an affordable entry is insane ... DIVE IN.

—Taylor Welch, founder of Welch Equities and WealthyConsultant.com, chairman of Traffic and Funnels, publisher of ConsultingMemo.com

If you have a message that *you know* matters, this way of speaking has the listener concluding it was *their* idea.

—**Kim Klaver**, 6-time top networking marketing producer, bestselling author of *If My Product's So Great How Come I Can't Sell It?*

The Million Dollar Speaker process is super simple. Any speaker—even complete newbies—can follow the system and start feeling accomplished instead of overwhelmed.

—**Angie Engstrom**, bestselling author of *Overcoming Mediocrity,* founder of the Vibrant Living Method

God *spoke* and the world was created. Throughout history, Elite Speakers have been the ones to change the world. You can learn their secrets of moving people to action with just your voice. Learn the system and stories, tips and techniques, bits and bonuses that the best of the best use to get rousing ovations and have a transformational effect on the lives of their hearers.

Boring speakers put their audiences to sleep. Elite Speakers invigorate their audiences and leave them begging for more. Become an Elite Speaker by incorporating the information in this book into your daily speech habits!

—**Donald Kubelka**, founder of ExpandoVision.com, Inc.

FOREWORD

It was almost 20 years ago the very first time I walked into my first seminar. I had no idea what to expect. I'd flown across the country, and it cost me a lot of money to get there. I didn't know anybody in the room, but I remember the nerves and anxiousness as well as the excitement as I sat down amongst a sea of people during the first presentation.

I didn't know how the speaking business worked, so when the first speaker got on stage, I was writing notes as fast as I could while he was giving his presentation. At the end of about 90 minutes, he ended up making an offer for the audience to buy his course. I was a little confused, but I remember watching as dozens of people jumped up and ran to the back of the room, each literally throwing $2,000 at him.

In fact, I remember sitting there doing the math: two people, then 10, then 20 ... I realized that in less than 90 minutes, this man had made over $50,000, which was more money than I'd made my entire life to that point. A few minutes later, the next speaker took the stage. At the end of his presentation, he sold a $5,000 offer. Once again, I did the math and realized that this man had made over $100,000 in less than 90 minutes.

My mind was blown and as I watched over and over again, the same thing happened over the next three days. I knew that this was a skill set I had to learn, no matter how shy or awkward I was. If some other human being like me could get on stage and make $100K in 90 minutes, I would dedicate my life to mastering that skill.

And I did. I spent the next decade of my life learning from the greatest stage presenters of all time. Learning how they do the presentations, how they use their trial closes, how they do the stack and the close. All the things that made them the best in the world. And I modeled them. And I practiced on stage after stage all around America and into other countries.

During the recession in 2008, live events stopped happening, so we transitioned from live stages to teleseminars and eventually from teleseminars to webinars. And I kept practicing my script over and over and over again until I eventually perfected it.

A few years later, I had a chance to speak at Grant Cardone's 10X event in front of 9,000 people where I was able to sell over $3.2 million in just 90 minutes, setting a world record for the most sales in the shortest period of time.

People ask me so much about what I did that I eventually wrote an entire book called *Expert Secrets*, showing my framework for how I do my presentations from stage and from webinars to close sales.

And I've got to admit that since I wrote *Expert Secrets* almost five years ago, I've continued to do presentations, and I've continued to learn little things here and there to make my presentations better. But for the most part, I haven't come across a big idea, a big aha, or big change for my presentations. Until earlier this year when I met Joe and Eileen. They had recently joined my Category Kings program, which is a relatively small group of people. They asked if they could share their new storytelling framework that they called B.I.T.S.

Obviously, I agreed and everyone in the room was excited to hear it. They stepped on stage here in Boise, Idaho, and I remember sitting back, hoping to learn one or two things I could add to my presentation, but not really having that much hope that there was something new that could increase my ability to sell from the stage that dramatically. As they started mapping out the B.I.T.S. system, the room was silent. You could only hear the scratch of everybody's pens writing as fast as they could on their notepads, including my own. To say that I was blown away is an understatement.

Everyone was so quiet that halfway through the presentation, Joe asked if we were getting it. And I remember raising my hand and saying, "I am so blown away by what you're saying, keep talking." In fact, they only had an hour on stage to present it and when they were done, I had them keep going 'cause I didn't want it to stop.

This process that they call B.I.T.S., where they unpack their Belief Identity Transformation System, is the most profound development in public speaking that I've seen in my 20 years on stage.

And I've studied every speaker, every speaking coach. What I learned from them was so powerful that the next day I started creating a new presentation to sell a product we've been working on. And then I did a webinar seven days later. As I was creating that webinar, I went back and forth with Joe and Eileen to make sure that I had the pieces for my B.I.T.S. correctly, that I understood it, and had it in the correct order.

Less than seven days later, I went live on a webinar in front of thousands of people. I used my perfect webinar script, weaving in their B.I.T.S. framework. In a short 90 minutes, we did over $2.5 million in sales from that product's very first webinar.

I'm not gonna lie. I wish I would've learned this prior to writing the book *Expert Secrets*. I've almost gone back to my publisher three or four times to see if I can do an updated version incorporating B.I.T.S. into it because it's that powerful a strategy.

So far they've only shared this principle in very small rooms with high-end speakers. This book is the first time that the general public gets to learn and implement this highly effective strategy. Don't dismiss this as "simple" or think, "Oh, this is easy." This is one of the most powerful speaking and persuasion techniques I've ever seen.

I'm excited for this book, so I can go back to my old automated webinars and rebuild the presentations with these B.I.T.S. weaved into them as well as create new presentations for all my companies following the same methodologies and frameworks.

Congratulations, Joe and Eileen. For not only being great speakers and being great at *teaching* speakers, but also creating a whole new way for me to reimagine getting people to move from stage.

—**Russell Brunson**
Co-Founder of ClickFunnels;
Author of *Expert Secrets*, *Dotcom Secrets*,
and *Traffic Secrets*

SECTION I
Start Here

"Of the modes of persuasion furnished by the spoken word there are three kinds. The first kind depends on the personal character of the speaker; the second on putting the audience into a certain frame of mind; the third on the proof, or apparent proof, provided by the words of the speech itself."

— *Aristotle*

QUICK CURTAIN SPEECH

This book was written as a collaboration between Joseph Aaron and Eileen Wilder. To eliminate confusion around point of view, it's safe to assume that Joe is speaking unless the chapter starts with "from Eileen."

You'll also know who's speaking if you happen to notice when Joe refers to his wife, Melody, or Eileen refers to her husband, Harrison.

We hope you enjoy the show!

1

CAN I GET AN AMEN?

> "I've learned that people will forget what you said, people will forget what you did, but people will never forget how you made them feel."
>
> — *Maya Angelou*

As we were watching a speech from one of our clients, we immediately felt it ...

The lack of energy in the room. The quietness of the crowd. The one-liners landing flat.

My business partner Eileen and I sat in stunned silence. We were both thinking the same thing: *I don't know what to say.*

I looked at Eileen. "He's struggling. We know how to move an audience, but how do we explain it to him? How do we tell him what it is we're doing when we're speaking?"

It wasn't just David. Some of our other students still weren't passionately moving their audiences. We were trying to help David adjust his delivery, but something was missing from our teaching.

I sat down with David after the event for a coaching session. I said, "David, you know how you are a successful podcaster?"

He nodded.

"You are very comfortable in the studio, but you're having a one-way conversation. You aren't used to feeling the energy of your audience as you're talking."

He seemed to be tracking.

"It's kind of like the difference between white church and black church. When I was growing up, my dad was the only white minister among 2,000 ordained black ministers in our denomination. In our church, there was an ebb and flow … a back and forth … a give and take.

"In black church, you're *expected* to respond. There are shouts of 'Amen!' and 'Preach it, brother!' But in white church, the sermon is delivered more like a monologue. No shouts from the audience. No one is getting up from their seats or getting loud. The message is a one-way conversation from the pulpit to the pews, and that's as far as it goes.

"Your presentation, David," I said, "is more like white church."

David gave me a blank stare. I couldn't tell if this was helping. I could feel the lack of clarity. I could tell by the expression on his face that my feedback still wasn't actionable enough.

We needed to teach him how to move his audience, but *how?*

Eileen and I decided we wouldn't rest until we figured out how to help David and our other students learn the art of persuasive presentations.

We started listening to hundreds of hours of speeches.

We became obsessed with what makes the greatest speakers great.

We'd go to YouTube, sort by the "most popular," and watch the best speeches that people ever gave. We studied Tony Robbins, T.D. Jakes, Joel Osteen, Dr. Martin Luther King Jr., JFK, and many others.

Suddenly, we started to discover the "moves" they were all making.

Patterns started emerging ...

And then, as if someone was peeling back the curtain ...

We saw it.

Every single famous speaker was using the same framework.

We were like, "Wait. Hold up. What? Why didn't anybody ever tell us about this pattern?"

Nobody ever explained this framework. Even when Eileen was going to Bible School to become a pastor, she never learned it. Her *job* was going to be speaking. But do you think anyone bothered to show her how to speak in a way that would move her audience?

I grew up watching pastors get their congregations fired up. But I just figured the audience would engage when the pastor told them to. "Can I get an AMEN?"

I never paid much attention to the patterns they were using. I never saw a framework emerge.

Until now.

Once Eileen and I discovered this pattern, we started teaching it to all of our students.

David learned it and applied it the next time he did a presentation. He came back to us and said, "Oh my gosh! You're not going to believe this! I started doing the framework the way that you taught us to do it. While I was presenting, a woman who was listening while driving said she had to pull her car off to the side of the road—get out of the car—and start running around because she was so excited!"

David took this woman to black church. He got it!

Can you imagine speaking in a way that makes your audience get *that* excited—excited enough not only to stop what they're doing but also to buy from you?

What if all you needed was a simple framework, and you'd be able to speak from stage and move the masses?

What if we told you that everything we shared with David is in this book?

And what if, by learning it and applying it, you could put yourself on the path to becoming a Million Dollar Speaker?

Well get ready, because once you have this skill, *everything changes.*

2

YOUR STAGE AWAITS — FROM EILEEN

> "Quit waiting to get picked; quit waiting for someone to give you permission; quit waiting for someone to say you are officially qualified ... and pick yourself."
>
> —Seth Godin

The pain of self-doubt was crippling. I had long relinquished my dream of speaking on big stages. Because the invitations never came, I figured ...

I should just lower my ambition.

Be more content.

Settle into what others expected of me.

For a person called to speak, however, the pain of not fulfilling that purpose can be utter agony.

For years, I waited to be invited onto other people's stages.

I figured it would happen in an act of divine providence, once I had earned the right, been tested of merit, done the "hard yards," and come out:

"Proven."

But for some reason, the invitations never came …

So I worked harder on my speeches. Devoted time to more study and research.

And even wrote a book.

When enough time went by with no invitations, I figured I must not be a speaker.

What I didn't realize was that I had subtly bought into the lie of:

Waiting to be picked.

Self-doubt eventually made its way into the living room of my mind and set up camp like an unwanted house guest.

I guess it wasn't meant to be, I reasoned.

Then one day, I was reading the words of Steven Pressfield in *The War of Art*[1]:

> Self-doubt can be an ally. This is because it serves as an indicator of aspiration. It reflects love, love of something we dream of doing, and desire, desire to do it. If you find yourself asking (and your friends), 'Am I

---

[1] Steven Pressfield, *The War of Art: Winning the Inner Creative Battle,* (London: Orion, 2003), p. 39.

really a writer? Am I really an artist?' chances are you are. The counterfeit innovator is wildly self-confident. The real one is scared to death.

And I felt something I hadn't sensed for years:

Hope.

Maybe I am a speaker? I thought.

I have a feeling you might be like I was and not be aware of how talented you really are. You may look at other speakers and think, *I'm not that well-spoken, I am not that eloquent, I am not that powerful. Why would anyone ever want to hear what I would have to say?*

If you have a sense you're called to share your message, may I encourage you?

Someone out there needs your story. The way you deliver it. The way you bring it to life. They don't need someone else's story—they need to hear how you made it through that trial. How you made it through that challenge. How you got your breakthrough.

The Scripture says: "My sheep hear my voice, and I know them, and they follow me" (John 10:27, KJV). There are people that you are meant to help, but they can't follow you if they don't hear *your* voice.

Too often, we don't speak up, because we are waiting for someone to tell us we can, to release us into sharing our message.

I remember listening to a preacher during this time of self-doubt in my own life, and he said something that arrested me:

Two-thirds of God's name is "Go."

He went on to say that so often we are waiting on God, but God is waiting on us. He is leading us through the desires that are in our hearts.

In fact, he explained the root word of "desire" in Latin is "of the sire," meaning "of the father."

Your *desire* to speak—to change lives—is of the Father.

It's God-given.

I began to see that I was waiting on God …

But God was waiting on me.

I felt like heaven leaned forward and whispered in my ear: "*Go.*"

From Uber Driving to Making $108,000 in a Single Day

Before my revelation, I was a *normal* person. I spent a lot of time at Target. I worked my day job and came home and watched Netflix. You know, *normal* stuff.

My husband and I had been associate pastors for 18 years at a church in Washington, DC, ministering to others day in and day out. We didn't make a lot of money. So when we transitioned from that church, my husband drove for Uber to support our family.

During that time, I attended a conference where I met a phenomenal speaker named Myron Golden, who would later become my mentor. I asked him to teach me all about speaking, and what this man taught me changed my life forever. Not just in business but in all aspects of my life—family, God, wealth, and financial stewardship.

I couldn't wait to get started!

With my newfound confidence, and my speech ready to go, I booked a small conference hotel room in Houston and hustled to sell tickets.

I sold eight. Man, was I pumped!

I was like, *Holy cow, eight people just bought my $47 ticket to come to my presentation! I'm nervous, but this is going to be amazing. Eight people trust me enough to come!*

As the days crept closer to the event, I started getting really anxious.

I invited some friends to come so the room would look even fuller (and I would look cooler), and I asked another friend to speak, so I wouldn't have to fill the whole event with content.

On the day of my presentation, I was nervous but excited. My audience was 12 people, but I showed up like I was Tony Robbins speaking to an arena of 20,000.

The event was filled with poignant moments, and everyone felt comfortable sharing their stories.

The event began to take on another dimension ...

Conversations turned into intimate coaching from peer to peer ...

The teaching was helping the attendees connect and encourage one another ...

The room was permeated with a safe, calming vibe, but at the same time palpable with expectation and new possibilities.

During a few moments when people got vulnerable (and shed a few tears), I thought:

I had no idea this was going to be so powerful.

I started seeing a principle of persuasion at work:

Immersion causes conversion.

The presentation *itself* was converting the minds of the attendees—toward higher-level thinking. And it was converting them to go deeper with me after the speech was over. They didn't want this feeling to stop.

During the event, I was overwhelmed with a sudden and almost sad awareness.

I never needed to be INVITED to speak ...

I could have created my OWN stage.

I never needed to WAIT to "become" a speaker ...

I can decide that I AM a speaker!

I don't need to be "knighted" or "ordained" to go change someone's life ...

I can create my OWN life-changing room.

My whole life, I had been waiting for speaking invitations to come knocking, but I discovered:

Speaking had been waiting on me.

And at the end of the two days, following the exact steps we're going to reveal to you in this book, I made $108,000.

That was quite a wake-up call! I was absolutely stunned. Awed.

Internally arrested, with the simplicity, ease, and joy of doing my own event.

My mind was racing. *You mean I can teach stuff I love to talk about with super positive listeners, then invite them to work deeper with me at the end? AND HAVE FUN?*

OMG. I'm in.

After the presentation, my friends and I sat on a rooftop restaurant at the Marriott Marquis, overlooking the Houston skyline. With a soaring feeling of confidence, control, and security, we knew we had discovered the one thing that could catapult our success and impact countless lives: transformational speaking.

You have permission.

Once you realize no one needs to qualify you … knight you … ordain you …

You can go ahead and get to work.

Once you realize that God is with you, the angels are cheering you on, and those you are called to reach are waiting for you …

You can get down to business.

There hasn't been a better time in history to have a "quantum leap," generate massive income, and change countless lives.

And the great news?

All the gatekeepers are gone.

It wasn't so long ago that to:

> Get a record deal …
>
> Publish a book …
>
> Create a TV show …
>
> Book an arena …

You needed major corporations to endorse you. Times have changed. Technology has changed. Now you can get direct access to the hearts and minds of millions with the phone in your pocket or the laptop sitting on your desk. Nothing is holding you back.

The time to start is now.

Cancel all contingencies.

Silence the fear that says:

> *What if it's the wrong thing?*
>
> *What if I mess it up?*
>
> *What if I don't finish?*
>
> *What if no one hears my thing?*

Who cares?

Here's the truth: There is no wrong way to start. Don't let fear hold you back.

Start before you're ready.

I love how author and motivational speaker Zig Ziglar says it: "You don't have to be great to start, but you have to start to be great."

If leap-frogging your way to 6- and 7-figure days while impacting people is what you desire, then congratulations ahead of time. You're in the right place! With the strategies outlined here, you'll be able to both captivate and activate your audiences.

In this book, you'll discover why Joe and I have decided to dedicate our consulting to helping businesses with the *one thing* that changes *everything*:

Speaking that excites audiences and moves them to action.

We have the privilege of sharing this message far and wide across the internet. I have even spoken on stage with some of our mentors, such as Russell Brunson and Myron Golden, who have revolutionized and catapulted our business into the millions.

And now we have the privilege of teaching it to you!

It's called the Belief and Identity Transformation System™, and it's the little hinge on which gigantic doors swing wide open.

3

WHAT'S POSSIBLE SEEMED IMPOSSIBLE

"It always seems impossible until it's done."

—Nelson Mandela

Before buying a golf-course mansion in sunny Florida, I struggled to pay the rent on a crowded townhouse less than a mile away. I can remember driving up to my apartment after a four-day trip to San Diego for a real estate training. There was yet another pink sheet on the front door. Eviction was looming.

How embarrassing. Now the neighbors all knew that I was late on my rent. Again.

It wasn't from lack of effort. I had been selling marketing services to real estate agents for years. But it wasn't getting me anywhere. As I snatched the eviction notice from my front door, I shook my head in frustration.

I couldn't stop thinking about the event I had just attended. During his presentation, the real estate trainer made an offer to all the agents in attendance. One by one, the relatively small room of agents stood up to deliver their paperwork and sign up for his special program.

My mind couldn't stop doing the math. He had collected over $360,000, and all he did was talk!

An entrepreneur at heart, I was working 50-75 hours per week, trying to increase the sales of my struggling businesses. My wife, happy to have me home from my travels, looked at me with a knowing glance as I walked in the door clutching that pink sheet of paper in my fist. We were all too accustomed to the threat of homelessness.

Years earlier, while trying to start a nonprofit movement for teenagers, we experienced homelessness three times as a family of five. Nothing scared us more than the threat of this possibility again. And nothing was more important to me than staying in my home.

Something needed to change.

How could I be working so hard in my marketing business yet making so little? This real estate guy talked for a few days and made more money in that short time than I could make in a few years.

I "knew" how to speak. I had been speaking to churches, nonprofits, and schools for years. I knew how to inspire, motivate, and even train crowds of people. But I had never made $360,000 from a speaking gig. Let's face it, I had never made $3,600 from speaking.

That event was my wake-up call.

I decided that if that guy could make $360,000 in a weekend from "talking real good," I could make that—and *more*.

Fast-forward 15 months ...

I was sitting in my office, my pen frozen in mid-air. I double-checked my math to ensure what had just happened. Earlier that day, I served as a speaker and organizer for an event where the guy I was helping made one million dollars in a single day. That's right: *$1M in a single day.*

There was no substantial energy spent to generate this sum. There was no hustle. No grind. We had simply addressed an audience on Zoom. It wasn't even a very big audience: 164 people on a Zoom call. And he made ONE MILLION DOLLARS in income. That's six zeros: $1,000,000.

I didn't scream. There was no happy dance. No celebratory jumping up and down. I sat in stunned silence, frozen, with my eyes wide and my hand over my mouth. Any outside observer would have assumed I was angry.

And I was. I was a little angry, to be honest. Excited about what had just happened, yes, but also deep in thought.

For at least 15 minutes after the Zoom call ended and I calculated the numbers, I sat there thinking, *What have I been doing?*

I considered the years—no, the *decades*—of hustle and grind and struggle and frustration ...

I considered all the courses and masterminds and trainings and networking meetings I had attended ...

I felt a lump in my throat as I remembered all the family moments missed, the fights about money, and the unnecessary drama I had put my family through as I fought to be the provider I wanted to be for my family.

And in ONE DAY, I helped generate an amount of money that would take the average family in America over a decade to earn!

This was getting insane. I was now singularly focused on becoming the kind of person who could speak well and move an audience to action. Little did I know what would become possible with that focus.

That 7-figure day was in early 2020, and in the few years that have followed, my business partner Eileen and I have seen what others would call "impossible" happen again and again.

Million dollar days for us became multi-million dollar days for our clients and fellow mastermind members.

We discovered how to use the spoken word in combination with an invitation to help our audiences. In this new world of speaking like a Million Dollar Speaker, anything is possible.

All you have to do is commit to focusing *only* on the things that will substantially move your dreams and purpose forward.

Put into practice everything we are about to share with you in this book, and you will be doing what almost no one else is doing: Giving your business a massive cash injection using the power of great speaking.

Once you do it a few times, you'll never go back to business as usual.

Speakers, entrepreneurs, business owners, creators, influencers, teachers, visionaries, and leaders: This book is for you. *But* this book will not be actionable *unless* you have made a few key decisions.

I've spent a lot of time helping speakers go from a dream of speaking on stage to regularly doing six-figure days with their speeches—even online. At the highest level, three core decisions must be made to skyrocket the Million Dollar Speaker into elite status.

Everyone, before they begin, must first *decide*.

What Does It Mean to "Decide"?

Like many new speakers, when I first started speaking for business, I was afraid to choose a specific audience. I didn't want to "limit myself." Needy for money, I didn't want to turn away a customer I could help.

But, the reality is that by serving everyone, I served no one. And without a clear, intended audience, I could not speak in a way that resonated with their circumstances.

I later learned that making a decision requires us to confront our tightly held beliefs concerning lack and abundance.

Other great thinkers have recognized the same conundrum. This conundrum is the fear of lack. I feared that by choosing a singular audience, I would be *losing* something.

Not limiting myself felt freeing to me, and deciding on a specific audience felt constraining. My unwillingness to accept limits became the steel bars of the prison of my mind, inhibiting my progress.

This is because of the very nature of making a decision.

Many years ago, reading a book by Tim Ferriss, I learned that the word "decision" comes from the Latin word "incision." Incision, of course, means "to cut." With the prefix "in," it means "to cut into." Decision, with the prefix "de," means "to cut off."

A decision means "to cut off" all other possibilities. Hence, my fear. The nature of a decision is that when you decide to do *one* thing, you are simultaneously choosing *not* to do an infinite number of other things.

This feeling of loss inherent in a decision will be front and center throughout your speaking career. Sometimes it will feel as if you're facing it at every turn.

Masterful communicators will tell you …

It's not what you put into a speech that makes it great—it's what you keep out.

The battle to make a decision, then, is constant. Decision-making is a massively underrated skill of immeasurable importance. We've distilled what could be an overwhelming process into three key decisions you need to make to elevate your speaking business.

Decision #1: Decide WHO You Will Serve

Once you have decided to speak, the next most logical decision is WHO do you want to speak to?

You'll find true freedom and a new level of growth when you pick a specific audience. This might feel like a big decision, but you are NOT limited to this audience forever. The audience I chose as my first audience is not the audience I serve exclusively today. But, I grew my skills and became a Million Dollar Speaker under that audience's tutelage.

So, pick an audience today. Ask yourself, "Who are the people that I will serve?"

Write down your answer:
_____

It doesn't have to be *the* answer. Just write down *an* answer. Stick with that audience for six months, and then assess if you should make changes from there.

Decision #2: Decide WHAT You Will Share

The second core decision of a Million Dollar Speaker is closely tied to the first one. Million Dollar Speakers must decide the end result that they are going to help their audience achieve.

New and aspirational speakers will often ask me if they need to know who to serve first or what they want to do first. There isn't a right answer. Some speakers know what they want to help people achieve first and then pick an audience from there. Some speakers pick an audience first and then choose exactly how to help them.

The order does not matter. But a decision must be made.

Those you choose to serve are at a certain place or benchmark in their lives. Your mission is to decide what you do to get them to a new place of identity or achievement.

As you will discover in great depth, for a Million Dollar Speaker, the transformation of those you serve is always front and center. It's a game changer.

A common, well-rehearsed model for stating what you do and who you serve is often called the "unique selling proposition" (USP), "refined marketing statement" (RMS), or "elevator pitch."

I do not want to belabor the idea, as it's sufficiently explained in countless other works. However, the ability to say what you do and who you serve is invaluable to your goals as a speaker.

Typically, it's taught as:

I help [WHO] achieve/do [WHAT] with/without [thing they want/thing they don't want].

For example, Eileen and I help entrepreneurs, business owners, and influencers do 6- and 7-figure days by hosting their own events and rocking the stage.

Decision #1 and decision #2 together should allow you to be able to simply say who you serve and what you help them achieve or become.

Don't be mediocre here. Communicate well.

Write your statement and memorize it.

I help _____ achieve/do _____ with/without _____.

This is critically important. Before you move to decision #3, stop reading and start writing. Even if you use voice to text, get the words down. You can't mold clay in your imagination. You've got to have something tangible to work with or it will never take shape.

Write. It. Down.

Decision #3: Decide to BE a Million Dollar Speaker

You want to help a *lot* of people to get results and experience transformation, right? Then it's important to notice that when you DECIDE to serve people, and you DECIDE to serve a lot of them, you are simultaneously deciding to BE rich!

Money was not really my initial, core motivator. Helping a lot of people was my mission. But I remember the day when I finally decided to be okay with making a lot of money (so long as I was also helping a lot of people). That decision happened in a bookstore where I was innocently reading a book, probably not unlike what you're doing right now.

The simple act of reading words on a page introduced new ideas that I chose to embrace, which led me to experience a transformation—a renewing of my mind. Everything radically changed after that.

5

WHY NOT SET AN ABSURD GOAL?

"The only thing worse than being blind is having sight but no vision."

—*Helen Keller*

Sitting in one of those big armchairs in a bookstore near the café, where people were ordering lattes and muffins, I was reading a book that I was too poor to buy. As in ... I never would have invested in the book because it cost too much money. I was *that* broke.

As I was reading, I got to this one page, very early on in the book, where the author, Tim Ferriss, asks billionaire Peter Thiel a question that has since changed my life:

"How do billionaires and high-achievers think differently than the rest of us?"[2]

Billionaires achieve seemingly superhuman feats—things that other people see as impossible—but they don't have superpowers. Their thought processes allow the bending of reality to such an extent that it may *seem* that way, but they've just

---

[2] Timothy Ferriss, *Tools of Titans: The Tactics, Routines, and Habits of Billionaires, Icons, and World-Class Performers* (New York, NY: Houghton Mifflin, 2017), p. xix.

learned how to adjust their way of thinking. So, how do they do it?

In response to Tim's question, Peter asks Tim how much money he would want to be making in ten years. I thought to myself, *A million dollars. In ten years, I'd like to be making a million a year.* I realized that's about $100,000 a month, and that sounded amazing—life-changing levels of amazing.

What Peter said next blew my mind. He shared the way that *he* thinks about that goal. And it goes like this: If you have a ten-year goal, ask yourself the question, *Why can't I do that in six months instead?*

I know it sounds super intense. Here's another analogy I like to use: If my kids were kidnapped and I couldn't get them back until I hit the goal, what would I do?

Real quick, I want you, in your head, right now, to tell yourself how much you would like to be making per month in ten years. Then, think about what you would need to do to adjust that goal to a six-month goal. This is the thinking of a super-achiever. This is how billionaires think. I know it sounds crazy—absurd, even.

But the power is in the absurd! The more absurd, the more "impossible" the question, the more profound the answers. Billionaires aren't that different from everyone else. They're world-class performers who are experts at relationship-building and networking. Anyone can do that with practice. But they *think* differently. Set absurd goals and you'll be thinking like a billionaire, too.

Standing there in that little bookstore, I slammed the book shut. I said to myself, *Wow. That was eye-opening. I need to go think about this.* And you know what? It didn't take me but a day to think through *exactly* what I would need to do to hit $100K per month. What changed?

My thinking.

I went to work and thought, *I'm going to crush this!* At the time, we weren't even making $2,000 a month. But I had the newfound confidence and mindset of a billionaire. They ask bigger questions. They develop uncommon habits. They're not afraid to think way, *way* outside the box of what your average person thinks of as "success."

I went to tell my wife. I said, "Hey, we're going to do $100,000 a month."

She's like, "Okay, babe. Yeah, that's great. Go get it. Yes, please. Absolutely! I want you to do it."

And I started telling other people about it. They looked at me kinda funny because I was living in an apartment, and I was usually late on rent and struggled to pay for anything beyond the bare necessities. But I kept telling more and more people because I wanted to have some accountability.

I went after it. I followed my plan to hit my goals. And within 45 days, I was already at $20,000 a month. I was ecstatic. It was a *huge* deal. $2K to $20K isn't an incremental step. It's a giant leap. A 10X leap.

How did I do it so quickly?

I first DECIDED to do it.

If you're not making the money you want, you must DECIDE to make a scary goal. If you've never made $100K in a month, that means you've never DECIDED to make $100K in a month.

If you haven't decided it, you probably haven't thought about it as a real possibility. Instead, it's an incremental thing that you've put off into the future. I want to encourage you to believe that you're capable of more than you think you are. Your potential is infinite.

But **you must decide that you're going to do it.** If you don't make the decision, all the other things that are comfortable and normal in your life will pull you away from becoming the person *you need to become* to *do what it takes* to achieve your absurd goals. You could even decide that you're going to do not only a $100K month, but a $100K day. Imagine what's possible with the power of a speech that can move an audience to action.

6

THE MASTER KEY TO GETTING ANYONE TO DO ANYTHING

> "It doesn't matter how elegant the argument or inspiring the prose, a presentation won't move anyone if the presenter isn't visibly feeling what they are saying."
>
> —John Neffinger

Imagine presenting in a way that compels your audience to spend $3 million in 30 minutes. That's $100K per minute. And that's what happened when Myron Golden, who is an absolute legend when it comes to speaking, spoke from the stage at Funnel Hacking Live the year before I met him. The power of this man's words moved thousands of people to spend thousands of dollars, generating an additional $3 million in sales for the event.

I was confident this guy had something to teach me. So I decided to join his high-ticket mastermind. Little did I know that it would be in this mastermind where I'd meet my future business partners, Eileen and her husband Harrison. It was a great decision.

I took my 14-year-old daughter Emily to the first meeting in Tampa, FL. It was about a three-hour drive from my home in Melbourne, FL, but Emily was already a professional speaker too, so it was going to be a lot of fun.

I was already effective at inspiring and connecting with audiences. But, I didn't have a great handle on how to operate inside the business and personal development settings. Many of the speakers in those arenas, in my experience, were pretty boring.

They'd have long powerpoints, relatively low energy, and very little crowd engagement.

I wondered if that kind of buttoned up, business-like, "ace" approach was what I'd need to grow a business from speaking.

I was no longer interested in speaking merely to inspire. I had been homeless enough times to realize that going broke and putting my family into financial hardship was not my chosen path to make the world better.

Ideally, I wanted to create an inspirational experience during speaking events that would truly help people and would also grow my business and customer base. Surely, I could have success without being boring.

As I sat in my chair furiously taking notes as Myron shared his wisdom, he said something especially poignant. (That's a big statement because Myron is *full* of wisdom.)

This one statement would change the direction of my focus and serve me in adding millions in revenue to my business over a few short years.

He stopped his pacing at the front of the hotel conference room, looked in my direction, and peeked over his glasses. He asked, "Do you wanna know how to get your audience to buy during your presentation?"

I nodded my head affirmatively and inched forward to the edge of my seat, pen in hand ready to write. Emily nudged me with her elbow. Smiling, she knew that this was what I came for.

"Here's the secret," he said. "Make them FEEL like buying."

I wrote it down and sat back in my chair. Feel? Now *that* was a word I could resonate with.

"You know what people do?" Myron continued. "People do what they *feel* like doing. They don't do what they don't feel like doing unless they're especially disciplined. They even do what they can't afford to do. If someone feels like buying a car and they can get the loan, what do they do?"

"They buy the car," everyone in the room responded.

"What about a BIG purchase like a house? If they can get the loan to buy the house and they feel like buying the house, what do they do?" Myron asked again.

"They buy the house," we all said.

"So if people are gonna buy what they feel like buying and move when they feel like moving … if you wanna make them move, all ya gotta do is to make them feel like doing the thing you want them to do next."

I let the truth of that simple statement marinate in my mind. I thought to myself, *All I gotta do is help them feel.*

Myron didn't know it at the time, but that little statement changed my life and the life of many of my future clients. The next logical question was, *How do I do that?*

What I did not realize at that moment was how central speaking is to most businesses today. Stages are no longer just raised platforms in a hotel room, church, or auditorium. In comparison with today's world, those stages are acutely limited.

It's no mistake that social media channels are called "platforms." The potential reach due to the advent of social media, along with live-streaming experiences from your phones, Zoom meetings, and more, has made the skill of speaking exponentially more valuable.

To make a sale, you obviously need something to sell. But again, before you ever get to the place where you can make an offer to purchase, you must have an audience's attention.

In today's world, that happens through speaking.

Whether you realize it or not, you are in competition with the whole world to capture someone's attention. The ability to gather a crowd, speak online, hold attention, and move your audience to either join your movement or buy your product or service—these are now some of the most valuable skills in the world.

Done well, you can gather the attention of hundreds of thousands or even millions in a matter of days. I've discovered that there is an interesting dichotomy, though, in how it's done.

There tend to be two distinctly different groups of speakers.

The first group is what I call the creators. They are great at creating good content that gets the world to pay attention, but creators tend to be weak at monetizing.

The second group is made up of entrepreneurs and marketers. This group tends to be good at monetizing an audience, but weak at capturing attention.

The skills you will learn in this book will allow you to speak in such a way that you capture the attention of your ideal audience while simultaneously increasing sales in your business, non-profit, community, or movement using the power of a simple "invitation."

We're gonna help you to make the audience FEEL in a way that's genuine, pure, and powerful.

There are three main problems people tend to have when they decide to speak to grow their business or movement:

1. They don't know where to speak.

2. They don't know what to say.

3. They don't know how to say it well.

We'll address all these concerns.

But first, I want to put number one to rest: you don't need a physical stage to speak from. There are now infinite platforms to speak from. The stage is in your pocket.

Everything we are about to share on what to say and how to say it to move your audience can happen on any stage.

It can happen in your Facebook lives. It can happen on your YouTube channel. It can happen in podcast interviews or in Instagram interviews with friends or colleagues.

We want you to GET LOUD on platforms everywhere. Pull out your phone and speak where your people are.

7

WHAT IS THE BELIEF AND IDENTITY TRANSFORMATION SYSTEM?

> "All you need is the plan, the road map, and the courage to press on to your destination."
>
> —*Earl Nightingale*

Are you ready to speak like a Million Dollar Speaker? Knowing what to say and how to say it well will serve you in every area of your life but especially as a speaker.

This book will become a resource that you'll come back to again and again as you build out your content using the system we're about to show you. Inside this system are the frameworks our Million Dollar Speaker clients use to rock stages everywhere and create 6- and 7-figure days.

It's taken us years to study the greats, dissect the world's best speeches, and discover a framework that applies repeatedly. We've organized it to follow the steps of our Belief and Identity Transformation System.

Without a systematic approach to convey truth that transforms, the messages tend to fall flat. That's a tragedy.

I'm convinced that some of the most powerful messages and some of the most transformational ideas in the world have never been heard.

Why? There are two likely possibilities:

First, and most likely, the person who holds those new ideas and messages is afraid to share them because they're not confident in how to communicate these valuable truths. If they had a framework, they might feel confident enough to share them.

Secondly, a brilliant thinker attempts to speak the truth but fails to convey the information in a way the audience can receive it. Truth ineffectively communicated is heard but not understood.

Both circumstances are tragic but avoidable.

This is why we created the Belief and Identity Transformation System.

Once you understand this system, you'll have a framework for knowing what to say, how to create your content, how to present your content, and how to invite your audience into the journey of transformation with you.

This will create a bigger following for you, larger donations to your nonprofits, greater status as a leader, and yes, greater income for your businesses and financial endeavors.

So what is the system?

- Step 1: LISTEN to your audience.
- Step 2: CREATE your content.
- Step 3: INVITE your audience on a journey.

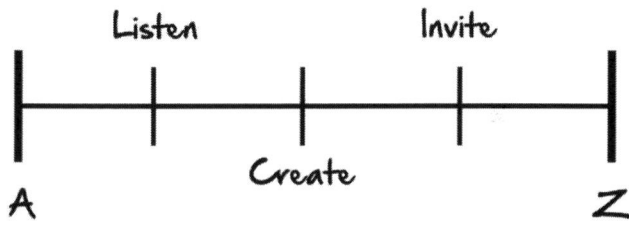

Step 1: Listen

In the first section, we will show you how to listen first. Your audience will tell you what to talk about. This will ensure your messages remain relevant. Speaking is not about making the speaker look good. It's about listening to the audience and delivering a transformative message.

While mediocre speakers are concerned about saying things well, they're not focused on saying the right things. Great speakers focus on and speak to the true desires and needs of their audience.

The world's greatest speakers are the world's greatest listeners.

Step 2: Create

In this section, we'll show you how to organize your content into a format that'll allow your audience to experience and feel the information, not just hear it. When we've shared this in the past, other communicators have had huge light bulb moments bout their own speaking, and they've crushed it in their next presentation.

Step 3: Invite

Most of the world's speakers miss this step. If they do *not* miss it, many get very awkward when it's time to make what we in the speaking world call "the pitch." There's no need to get weird. In this section, we'll show you the kinds of offers you should be making, the context for making those offers, and how to present the offers so they feel great to everyone.

Once you organize your content following the Belief and Identity Transformation System (which we'll discuss in the next section), your world *changes*. Your influence, impact, and income all can soar to new levels when you master this framework.

Are you ready to become a Million Dollar Speaker?

SECTION II
The System

"If you are working on something exciting that you really care about, you don't have to be pushed. The vision pulls you."

—Steve Jobs

8

FIND OUT WHAT'S HOLDING YOUR AUDIENCE BACK — FROM EILEEN

"Knowledge speaks, but wisdom listens."

—Jimi Hendrix

The words were flowing out of her like a mighty river of power. The audience, in a state of hypnotic attention, was leaning forward, eyes wide open, hanging on her every word.

Children were leaning in, grown men gripped by her oratory. You could hear a pin drop.

Pacing across the platform, her voice was filled with authority and command. As she spoke, describing their pain, their frustrations, and their fears—you could feel it.

They felt known.

Understood.

Seen.

The most beautiful feeling started permeating the atmosphere:

Trust.

How is she doing that? I wondered. *It's as if she knows them better than they know themselves.*

She knew them well because she was acquainted with her audience's struggles and pain, thanks to her listening skills. And she was telling *their* story from the stage, not hers.

Focus on Them, Not on Yourself

Too often, speakers are focused on telling their *own* story; they miss the opportunity to tell the story of their audience.

And while your own story will be powerful content for your presentations, incorporating the words your audience is feeling will help them quickly say, "Wow, this speaker *really* understands what I'm going through."

Your speech will be even more potent if you talk to *one* person in the audience. Describe their struggle better than they can even articulate it to themselves. Communicate their emotions, their experiences, and their aspirations. They will think: *I feel like they're talking directly to me.*

By focusing on them and not on yourself, your presentation is now serving the audience at the highest level because you're earning their trust, which is the most precious asset they have to give you.

How Do You Get Inside Their Head?

The world's greatest speakers don't assume they know what their audience is thinking—they actually know. They're well acquainted with their ideal client's biggest fears, their inner

…urmoil. They know exactly what's keeping their listeners up at night, what they're worried about, and what struggles they're facing.

So how do they do it? How do they know their audience so well? More importantly, how do YOU find out what pain and problems your audience is facing?

The key isn't speaking. It's listening.

The best way to discover what your ideal clients are struggling with is by asking some real, potential clients what their biggest struggles are and then getting quiet. Let them do the talking.

The best speakers are the best listeners.

Your goal here is to have conversations with at least three people you feel could embody an ideal client. Or if you have favorite customers—pick up the phone and talk with them.

These could be casual conversations over a coffee or even over the phone or Zoom. Your goal is to be an excellent, compassionate, and focused listener. Let the other person do most of the talking.

Don't worry about following a rigid "customer research" formula.

Your objective is to get good at asking questions that help you truly understand your customers' needs, frustrations, and desires. Not only will this help you develop the best presentation possible, but you'll also have the insight to present the perfect invitation to your audience when you deliver your message.

This is because you'll know the exact language to use to describe what your customers are going through and what they want.

The most important thing to focus on is being present in your one-on-one conversations. Be interested in the human being you're talking to. Remember, there's no sales or business technique out there that can replace legitimate caring.

Get resourceful about finding three people to meet with, and then use the following questions as your guide. Pay attention and take notes. As Bob Burg says, "Sometimes the most influential thing we can do is listen."

Ideal Audience Questions:

Tell me about your life right now. What are your favorite parts?

You're looking for the basics—where they live, their job, marital status, do they have pets, kids, hobbies, and what's great about their life.

I'm working on a new idea for a presentation on _____ [fill in with your topic] and I'm curious …

What is the #1 question you have about trying to achieve X?

What do you feel is your #1 challenge in accomplishing X?

Based on their response, you might follow up with something like this:

That makes sense. Tell me more about why that's important to you …

What is the baby step you'd like to achieve right now?

Remember to honor the time you've allotted for this conversation and send a follow-up thank you card or email.

Identify Their Primary False Belief

Once your interviewees share their struggles with you, begin looking for a pattern.

What's the *biggest* obstacle they are facing?

What is *repeatedly* showing up in their answers?

What is their *common* challenge, even if it's worded slightly differently?

This is how you identify their #1 false belief that you will be focusing on in your presentation.

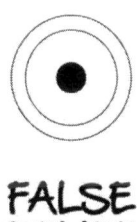

You Found Their #1 Challenge. What's Next?

Understand that you have already done what *most* speakers never do: listen and research their audience's fears, challenges, and roadblocks. Now that you've found their biggest false belief, your entire message will be focused on setting your audience free forever from the shackles that are binding them.

With this valuable information, you will know exactly what problems to address in your presentations. Not only will this transform their life forever, but it will also perfectly position them to be ready with an enthusiastic "YES" when you make your invitation.

But before you can think about inviting them to take the next step with you on a journey of transformation, you've got to start with where they are now (in their mindsets) and paint a clear picture of where they're going. You'll take them from their biggest struggles to their greatest dreams, all with the power of the spoken word.

> "Always enter the conversation already occurring in the customer's mind."
>
> —Dan S. Kennedy

9

THE POWER OF POLARITY

"The greater the contrast, the greater the potential. Great energy only comes from a correspondingly great tension of opposites."

—Carl Jung

When Oprah has to go to an unplanned commercial break to calm the audience down, you know her guest has some super secret magic sauce to share ...

A few years ago, I was watching Bishop T.D. Jakes promote his new book during an interview with Oprah Winfrey. The Bishop wasn't standing behind a lectern. He and Oprah were seated side by side on stage.

The in-studio audience, as part of a televised experience, was not meant to get loud, much less rowdy. But, if you don't want things to get wild, don't bring in a Million Dollar Speaker like T.D. Jakes.

Oprah was out of her seat yelling and pointing her finger. The audience was jumping up and down. And Bishop Jakes couldn't even finish his sentences without the audience hollering back in agreement.

What's more astonishing, he started all of this in response to a question. It didn't even seem like he planned this material …

"We gotta go to a commercial break," Oprah yelled into her microphone, trying to talk over the noise of the audience as her staff scrambled to an unplanned break.

I don't think this had ever happened on *Oprah* before.

I was astonished. My man just shut down *Oprah*. What could someone possibly do to elicit that kind of response?

In the past, when I would speak, sometimes I struggled to get the training just right. My content was good, but nothing transformative. Big surprise, my close rates for sales weren't all that great. They were just kind of average. I always felt like something was missing.

Then I discovered what I call "the secret of the two identities." That's when *everything* changed. All of a sudden, I had a scream-and-holler, high-five, back-and-forth, connected, loving-it audience—whether or not they bought anything—all because of the two identities.

Using two identities is how Bishop T.D. Jakes excited his audience to the degree that he shut down Oprah. And it's the overarching paradigm shift that's going to cause all your presentations to be more persuasive and experiential.

The Secret of the Two Identities

Think about your event as a timeline. People come in one way (Old Identity) and they leave a different way (New Identity). During your event, they should experience a complete identity shift. Your goal is to help people take a journey from their Old Identity to their New Identity.

When they come in, they have a specific set of beliefs anchored to their identity. These are the underlying beliefs hidden behind their stated obstacle. In the previous chapter, we identified the words they use to communicate the obstacles holding them back from their desired result. Behind these stated obstacles are underlying beliefs.

For example, if they state that "I don't have the money to start a business" as the obstacle holding them back from being a successful entrepreneur, there are beliefs behind that stated obstacle.

These limited beliefs are like invisible chains that are holding them back from becoming the person they're destined to be.

In this example, the beliefs behind that stated obstacle could be ideas such as:

- It takes a lot of money to start a business.

- Accessing money to start a business is hard or impossible.

- It takes money to make money.

Your job is to identify what thoughts (or beliefs) are holding them back. What are their fears? What are the assumptions that are preventing them from reaching the New Identity on their own?

Think about some of the false beliefs people have about getting to the New Identity (whatever that may be):

- how hard and complicated it will be
- the amount of time it will take them
- the technology that's required
- the amount of money they need to make it happen

Name all your false beliefs and write them down to understand the characteristics of what we call the Old Identity.

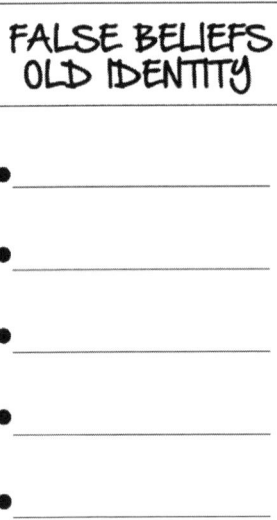

Now, let's skip to the end of your event. What new ideas and beliefs do they need to have so that they're the kind of person who will go all-in on themselves to get the result that they truly want? That's what you will write down under New Identity.

For example, Eileen and I might want our audience to be fast action-takers because we know that wealth loves speed.[3] We want people who are not procrastinators because "do it now" is one of the secrets to wealth. We want people who believe that high-ticket offers are the fastest and best path for them.

If there is anything you want someone at your event to believe, whatever those beliefs are, write them all down. And anything you want your audience to *not* be or represent, write that down, too.

```
EMPOWERING BELIEFS
    NEW IDENTITY
```

- _____
- _____
- _____
- _____
- _____

And here's the cool part: Now we get to name the identities and create a story for the audience.

---

[3] Russell Brunson, "Wealth Has A Need For Speed (With Special Guest Myron Golden!)," Apple Podcasts, *The Marketing Secrets Show*, October 5, 2020, https://podcasts.apple.com/us/podcast/wealth-has-a-need-for-speed-with-special-guest-myron-golden/id1315130618?i=1000493621670.

How We Incorporate the Identities in an Event

To help audiences self-select, using clear contrasts they resonate with, I will often tell a story of two identities in my own life called "Broke Joe and Woke Joe."

Two quick notes about the silly names I gave myself for these stories. First, these identities are in no way a measure of my value as a human; rather, they are ways of thinking. Second, "woke" did not have political connotations when I originally started using it.

In the event, I tell stories about how, when I was jobless and homeless, I was "Broke Joe." But after I started crushing it with virtual events, I became "Woke Joe." This was the version of me who had an awakening about what my life could be. I put my self-limiting beliefs in the past and awoke to a new reality of infinite possibility.

One false belief that I often help the audience tear down during an event is, "I don't have sufficient money or resources to execute my plan." Average speakers will merely tell the audience, "You've got everything you need; don't worry about it." But that won't work. The audience won't believe they have everything they need. Telling them that won't help them change.

Instead, I'll use the two identities of Broke Joe and Woke Joe to get the audience to decide to BE resourceful and believe that they DO, in fact, have the resources they need. Here's how I do that:

I'll list out the beliefs and excuses Broke Joe might have:

"I don't have enough of a team."

SECTION II: THE SYSTEM

"I don't have enough time."

"I don't have enough money for ads."

"I don't have the right technology."

When the excuses begin to surface in the event, through participants' questions and comments, I'll say:

"Let me ask you a question. Is that Broke Joe thinking or Woke Joe thinking? That's Broke Joe thinking, right?"

They'll tell me the answer in the comments of the virtual event or yell out the answer live in person. Then I'll contrast Broke Joe thinking with Woke Joe thinking by saying:

"Well, what does Woke Joe believe? Woke Joe believes, 'I have everything I need.' Woke Joe says, 'I don't lack resources. I lack resourcefulness. In my network, I have access to all the money I need, all the partnerships I need, all the connections I need.'

"Broke Joe blames. Woke Joe is resourceful.

"Broke Joe says, 'My potential is limited, this may not be possible for me.'

"But Woke Joe says, 'I can do anything I put my mind to. I am made in the image of God. I am a creator. And if I don't even have a solution yet, I can create one.'"

Finally, I'll ask them:

"Who do you want to be? Do you want to be Broke Joe? Or do you want to be Woke Joe?"

What I have done is contrast these two mentalities. Whenever I need to overcome objections, false beliefs, or ideas people have, I don't tell them what to think. I tell them the story about Broke Joe. Then I can tell the story of Woke Joe. How he achieved results, and how, despite the fact that he didn't have the resources, he *found* the resources and made it possible. And now his dreams are coming true.

So, using the stories of the two identities, you paint a picture for the audience and then ask them which identity they want to be.

You say to the audience:

"Do you want to be Broke Joe or Woke Joe?"

And the audience will yell or type back:

"Woke Joe!"

The audience is telling YOU who they decided to believe. They're shouting it at you now. This ingrains the belief exponentially deeper because you did not depend on merely telling them what to think. They're telling *you* who they want to be and how they want to operate.

SECTION II: THE SYSTEM

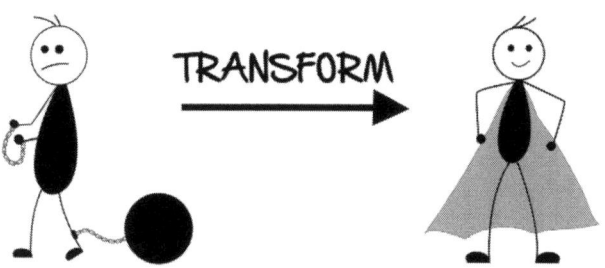

Are you starting to see the power of the two identities?

When you understand and implement the two identities, you will instantly unite your audience, fire them up, and take your event to a whole new level.

10

TRANSFORMATION SECRETS OF THE WORLD'S GREATEST SPEAKERS: EPIPHANIES, IDENTITIES, AND DECLARATIONS, *OH, MY!*

> "The first commandment of speaking: Don't be boring."
>
> —Unknown

This particular speech was NOT going well. People were fading FAST.

One man started drifting off to sleep, sliding silently into the personal space of the woman sitting beside him. As she jerked her shoulder away, the man quickly wiped some drool from his mouth and pretended to be fully present, looking around to make sure no one else noticed.

The speech could have—and should have—held the audience's attention.

The speaker had generated millions of dollars in real estate in a very short amount of time and was sharing a detailed and tactical approach to exactly how he'd achieved this phenomenal result.

Talk about the nuts and bolts … this could've been the mundane training manual for his team's daily activities.

All the attendees just needed to take notes, then take action, and they would potentially earn millions of dollars!

Unfortunately, transferring valuable information does not equate to a speech that actually changes an audience.

This is the fatal flaw and belief of mediocre speakers everywhere—they believe good information makes a good speech. But that's not enough.

Mediocre speakers focus on conveying information.

Million Dollar Speakers focus on orchestrating transformation.

This is a fundamental distinction. The contrasting experience of a typical presentation compared with that of a Million Dollar Speaker is palpable. This is because the Million Dollar Speaker's mission is not information—it's *transformation*.

Great speakers place their audience at the center of every speech, whereas mediocre speakers make information center stage.

SECTION II: THE SYSTEM

MEDIOCRE SPEAKER VS. MILLION DOLLAR SPEAKER

For the Million Dollar Speaker, content is merely a springboard from which new identities can be formed and declared.

Transformation happens when attendees enter the speaking event with one set of beliefs, values, and assumed identities, and then walk away from the event with a new set of values, beliefs, and identities.

Stop Informing. Start Transforming.

When most people are trained to speak, their main goal is applause. To paraphrase author and marketing legend Dan Kennedy, "All speaking to get applause is pandering."

There's a distinction between speaking for applause and speaking to create transformation in someone's life.

The difference between what Eileen and I teach and almost everyone else that we've studied is that we're focused on creating a transformational experience for the people who are in attendance at our events. We believe that each person should leave an event completely changed—whether they buy or not.

We'd love to show you how to do that. It doesn't do anyone any good for you to just give your audience content as everybody else does. Overloading them with information doesn't serve them at the highest level. What they need isn't more information, but transformation.

Of all the things a speaker might focus on, why focus on the transformation of the individual?

This is a very important question.

It's not intuitive for a speaker to think of transformation as a key metric of speaking success. But when you place the focus of your presentation on *transformation*, the entire context changes. Your audience becomes the subject, not some other extraneous topic. It's all about them, and they can FEEL it.

While there are numerous reasons to make the transformation of the individual central, the obvious one is because the most interesting topic to humans is "me." People in the audience come to hear a speaker, thinking, *What's in it for me?*

When the subject *is* your audience, they will experience your content in a deeper, more personal way. Allowing your audience to feel the effects of the content while you're talking makes your content relevant and interesting.

Make your audience the focus, and the delivery of your content will become a unique and engaging experience. It is through this experience that your audience will reach a new epiphany, shift their identity, and make a declaration.

There are three levels of transformational speaking.

The first level is the epiphany, where you get your audience to believe something new about the world around them.

The next level is the identity shift (as in the Broke Joe/Woke Joe example). At this level, you want your audience to adopt a new belief about themselves.

And the third level is the declaration.

At this point, your audience is not only believing conceptually but also declaring emotionally what they believe.

Level 1: The Epiphany

The first time I really started to understand the concept of transformation was while studying well-known author and entrepreneur Russell Brunson, who later became a friend.

Russell introduced an idea called an epiphany, which is a great word choice.

Merriam-Webster defines an epiphany as:

> (1): a usually sudden manifestation or perception of the essential nature or meaning of something
>
> (2): an intuitive grasp of reality through something (such as an event) usually simple and striking
>
> (3): an illuminating discovery, realization, or disclosure
>
> **b:** a revealing scene or moment[4]

---

[4] *Merriam-Webster.com Dictionary*, s.v. "epiphany," accessed August 7, 2022. https://www.merriam-webster.com/dictionary/epiphany.

In his book *Expert Secrets*, Russell Brunson says, "If you want people to adopt a new concept and want to get their buy-in, you have to lead them to the answer, but you can't GIVE it to them. They have to come up with the idea themselves. You plant the idea in their minds with a story, and if THEY come up with the answer, they will have sold themselves. The buying decision becomes theirs, not yours."[5]

This is Level 1 of transformation. When you experience an epiphany, you see the world through a new lens. New opportunities emerge, and old obstacles are instantly obliterated.

If you've ever experienced it, it feels like a massive dopamine hit to the brain. This enlightened perspective is filtered through an innumerable host of previous experiences, and your newfound understanding allows you to see the world differently.

Mediocre speakers usually don't create epiphanies. They only convey information.

Million Dollar Speakers help their audiences experience epiphanies, which can feel like the joy of a home-cooked meal or the elation of winning a game. The better the feeling, the more the audience wants it. To them, it feels like personal growth.

An epiphany helps your audience see the world differently. It's a transformational experience, but only at the belief level about the nature and reality of the outside world. You'll want to take the epiphany to a higher level of thinking.

---

[5] Russell Brunson, *Expert Secrets: The Underground Playbook to Find Your Message, Build a Tribe, and Change the World,* (New York, NY: Morgan James Publishing, 2017), p. 92.

If epiphanies do not become identities, you've only changed the data in the listener's brain. What you're after is not simply a revelation about the outside world. Your goal is to shift their identity.

Level 2: Identity Shift

Again, the epiphany from Level 1 can only get the audience excited about new opportunities and change their false beliefs about the world around them.

But as a Million Dollar Speaker, I don't just want my audience to believe something different about the reality of the world. I want them to believe something different about *themselves*. Remember Woke Joe/Broke Joe? Those are two completely different identities.

If you're giving a speech to a group of people who love to sail, but they have always believed the world is flat, they might envision themselves falling off the earth if they sail too far. They're limited by their false belief. They aren't yet capable of making the Level 2 identity shift from "I love to sail in the safety of the bay" to "I'm a world-traveling, sailing adventurer!"

We now need to convert that newfound truth (the earth is round) into a revelation of new identity, shifting them from people with limited beliefs to people whose beliefs bring freedom and possibility.

Content allows for epiphany but application allows for capability.

You must help the audience members draw their own conclusions about who they want to be on the basis of this newfound truth. If they decide to be a different version of themselves as a result of the epiphany, then they will truly change. Why? Because people will act in accordance with how they view themselves.

Therefore, the audience needs both an epiphany *and* a new identity.

Another way to frame the difference between Level 1 and Level 2 is by exploring the distinction between "doing" and "being."

Most people are just working on the "doing" but not working on the "being." Being comes first. If you don't "*be*" it, you won't "*do*" it. The goal should be to help each person in your audience **become** the kind of person who will then make decisions to do things that are aligned with the end result they truly want.

In the Bible, this process is called *metanoia*, which is an Ancient Greek word that means: changing of mind.

If you don't actually create **a change of mind in your audience**—changing their beliefs about their IDENTITY and what they're capable of—they're not actually going to do the thing you're teaching them to do. They're certainly not going to give it the same value and emphasis or present it in the same sequence that you do.

People must become who they need to become before they'll actually do what they need to do. Doing follows being. *Always!*

So the question is this: How do I create this metanoia experience that helps people become who they need to become?

One of the things that is important to help people get to their desired result is to recognize the obstacles in their identity that are holding them back from who they really want to be.

People don't want the external stuff. What they really want is to become the kind of person that's **worthy** of the external stuff.

When I got an award for the first time I made a million dollars, I cried. I mean, *I cried* when I got that award.

I didn't cry because I earned a million dollars. I cried because I had finally *become* the kind of person who could achieve such a feat. It wasn't this prideful ego thing. It was actually quite the opposite.

I became someone different in the process. It was very humbling to realize all the ways that I had failed to live to my highest ability, in my highest purpose, and to my highest potential ... All the years I had wasted chasing the external things when it wasn't the external things I needed to succeed.

I needed to *become* someone different.

And when I became someone different, it happened so fast that it was like I almost didn't recognize myself ...

When the award came, I remember seeing myself in the mirror and realizing who I had become. Something broke inside of me. Suddenly, I felt a sadness that I hadn't become *him* before. But, there was also a joy and expectation for what was going to come as a result of being worthy of the external things.

And for everyone that hears me speak and for everyone that hears you speak, this identity transformation is what we want for them.

We want something to break inside of them.

I call it "speaking to the soul."

We want a recognition to take place inside of their spirit that says, *I'm called to a higher purpose. I'm capable of bigger things. What are these obstacles and lies and stories I'm telling myself that are keeping me from the highest order of everything I'm supposed to be doing?*

The Bible says that if something is set apart, it means to be *made holy or to sanctify it.* And people might not see speaking events as a way to cause people to be "set apart," but that's what happens when someone honors you with their time. When they're willing to set aside time to be with you, it is a holy moment. It is an "other moment" in their life. Completely *other* where they're saying, "This is the moment where I'm trying to become *who* I need to be in order to *do* what I'm called to do, so I can *have* what I ultimately desire to have."

But you have to be 100% all-in on caring about a ticket holder who is your potential client. You have to care enough to really bring the heat, to really bring the love, and to *honor* and be *holy* with that set-apart time. Really get into their life and say, "I need to talk past the mind, past the heart. I need to speak to the soul of what's really holding you back from everything you're supposed to be."

That is what an event is all about.

To speak to the soul, though, you have to avoid doing what most speakers have a tendency to do. Most speakers think, *I'm going to give them exactly what they need.* Then they'll launch into a presentation full of valuable *information*. But that's one of the worst things they could do, and it's probably the biggest mistake I see when people do events.

For example, if a speaker helps people lose weight, and an attendee wants to lose 20 pounds, a typical speaker will merely teach a weight-loss plan. They'll teach the audience to stop eating sugar, stop drinking soda, and have a diet plan.

This solely information-based approach is why the offer doesn't convert well.

Everybody is saying that. The audience thinks, *I know if I stop eating Twinkies, I'm probably gonna drop some pounds! No duh!*

Right? We know that lack of information about Twinkie calories isn't the issue.

The issue is deeper than that.

Why are *they* not changing their eating habits based on that information? That's the real question!

What if, instead, you spoke to their soul and started helping them get clear on what they truly desire? They would start imagining themselves in the future. They might think, *I want to be active enough to play sports with my kids through their high school years. I want to have the energy to rock climb and kayak and ski. I want my wife to think I'm handsome and sexy.*

Those are the identity desires.

Often we go to tactics. Speakers think that people need tactics or checklists, but what people really want, what they're crying out for, and what they're craving is for someone to help **transform** them into becoming the kind of person who will execute that plan.

While we do teach strategies and tactics when we speak at our events, we spend 80% of our work helping to **transform** people into who they really want to become. They want someone to help them with metanoia.

To summarize, at Level 1 you helped them question the fabric of reality and uncover new information about the world around them.

At Level 2 you helped them identify that they were making decisions based on what they had believed about themselves. Then, they decided to BE a version of themselves they truly wanted to be.

Now, you can move to Level 3.

Level 3: The Big Declaration

Remember, when Million Dollar Speakers speak, they carefully phrase their ideas to create epiphanies (moments of revelation). Epiphanies open the audience to the possibility of a new identity. Next, Million Dollar Speakers help audiences identify who they want to be and declare to the world their newfound identity.

Myron Golden, my speaking coach who I mentioned earlier, explained to me that my mission was to have my audience repeat my presentation back to me.

Why?

Because when *I* say it, they doubt it. They challenge it.

But when *they* say it, they believe it.

This is the trajectory of transformation.

By proclaiming it out loud, this declaration will cause audience members to truly experience the results they desire.

People believe 97% of what they say and 3% of what you say. (Why only 97%? That's because people lie to themselves. We can't even trust ourselves to always tell the truth!)

This is the way Million Dollar Speakers help the audience formulate their thoughts—their mental syntax.

Let's get ready to learn the framework for how to do this!

11

DISCOVER THE HIDDEN FRAMEWORK USED BY THE WORLD'S MOST PERSUASIVE SPEAKERS — FROM EILEEN

"If I went back to college again, I'd concentrate on two areas: learning to write and to speak before an audience. Nothing in life is more important than the ability to communicate effectively."

—*Gerald R. Ford*

The crowd was going crazy. People were standing, shouting, waving their hands, absolutely losing their minds. The atmosphere was thick with expectation, excitement, and the feeling that *anything* was possible …

The speaker was on fire, his words pouring out with passion, authority, and ease …

The noise from the crowd was almost deafening but in the best way.

You know how when you go to a concert to see your favorite band, and everyone is lost in the lyrics—together?

Here, now, the communicator and the crowd had formed an invisible partnership, feeding and fueling each other, lost in the lyrics of profound oratory ...

The arena was electric.

It was stunning.

It was like watching something superhuman.

Something other-worldly.

It was transcendent.

I looked back at the speaker and only one question permeated my mind:

How is he doing that?

That question has gripped Joe and me for years as we have watched speaker after speaker and analyzed event after event.

Why is the arena going crazy, now?

How did she command the audience so effortlessly, then?

Why did the sudden applause occur at that moment?

What we discovered shocked both of us. There was a pattern. A framework they were using. The best part?

It could be learned.

Use This Speaking Pattern to WOW Your Audience

The next few chapters may be the most important chapters you read in the entire book. I'm not exaggerating when I say that if you can master this *one thing*, you can not only transform your own life but also countless other lives.

We've seen it happen over and over with our students. They go from little to no engagement on their social posts and live videos to—all of a sudden—tons of comments, likes, and shares. Perfect strangers are joining their workshops and challenges. It's like flipping a switch.

Our clients call us and tell us how their audience engagement has gone through the roof. They're crushing it without putting in any more hours, without adding any more coaching calls or Q&A calls. Seemingly without effort, they're seeing their conversions go up exponentially.

By understanding and implementing the framework we're about to show you, you too will see results, almost overnight.

Once you learn the framework and start listening to speeches, presentations, podcasts, YouTube videos, and other speakers, you will be amazed, like us, to learn that:

Almost *no one* is doing this.

If you can master the art of this framework, you will have a massive advantage over your competition. In fact, you won't even have competition. I mean, who can compete with the greatest speakers of all time?

How Not to Be Boring

Remember at the beginning of this book when we told you that Joe and I became obsessed with listening to hundreds of hours of speeches? Once we discovered the pattern that every single great orator used, we needed to come up with a name for what they were doing so we could teach it to our students.

Two of my favorite comedians, Jerry Seinfeld and Jimmy Fallon, refer to content that lands well with their audiences as "bits." They throw out the bits that don't work and keep the ones that generate lots of laughs and big reactions for their routines.

Bits. I liked it.

Similarly, Joe and I have had lots of practice delivering content to our audiences. We've hosted dozens of virtual events and we've been invited to speak on multiple stages, so we've started paying attention to which of our bits land well and which ones flop.

Over the past few years, we've collected a treasure trove of carefully curated bits that almost instantly transform our attendees' thinking. They contain the right amount of emotional juice, humor, and logic to dethrone any false beliefs our audience has.

They are like sniper stories that could take out limiting beliefs faster than we can say **Belief & Identity Transformation System**, and that's exactly what they are.

Belief and Identity Transformation System (aka Bits)

Speaker Bits are like kryptonite for false beliefs. They subtly weaken the belief that's holding your audience back.

When you take your carefully crafted bits and place them into the framework that you're going to learn in the next chapter, you'll find that you suddenly have a mechanism to move your audience to greater heights than you could have ever asked or imagined.

Tested on stages throughout history by the greatest speakers of all time, bits have the power to move audiences like nothing else.

Without bits, your presentations will be boring. With bits, you'll feel the energy and excitement rise. You'll move audiences to their feet. You'll activate transformation. You won't just poke a hole in their false beliefs—you'll completely obliterate them.

Right now, your ideal audience is walking around with invisible chains tethering them to their old identity. With each bit, you shoot an arrow of truth that unlocks one chain of many, helping to free them from the imprisonment of their false beliefs.

What false beliefs are holding your audience captive? What must they believe to become the person who can achieve the results they currently only dream of? Those are the ingredients for your pieces of content—your best bits.

Our bits often challenge a traditional, uncontested idea that the audience has typically believed their whole life, because society, school, or social pressure has told them to believe or act a certain way. Things like: Go to college. Get a job. Save your way to wealth. Work until you're 65 so you can make a lot of money.

They are anesthetized to the compromised position they are in.

And as Million Dollar Speakers, we are here to wake them up—to present a NEW way to look at who they REALLY are, and what they are really capable of.

When you master the bits system, your presentation will seamlessly embed the core beliefs that you want your audience to adopt by the end of the event. You'll be able to capture your audience's attention and instill in them the desire and need for what you have to offer.

With each bit, you're telling a story. We'll get to what we call the "bit barrage," but for now, let's focus on what a bit is and how it can help ignite a fire within your audience.

What Is a Bit?

A bit is an intentionally crafted flow of content that delivers an important point with coordinating one-liners and soundbites. It's designed to free your audience from the cords that bind them and release them to what's possible with the truth.

A successful bit plants the seed of a thought into the mind of your listeners. As you water that thought throughout your presentation, it will grow, and your audience will think it, believe it, and speak it. When your audience goes from hearing *your* message to speaking *their* message, that's when true transformation takes place.

And that's the goal. You might be living in the information age, but you're in the transformation business.

12

PRESENTING WITH POWER: HOW TO USE SPEAKER BITS TO MAKE A POINT, ATTACK A FALSE BELIEF, AND SHIFT THINKING

> "Never tell a story without making a point. And never tell a point without a story."
>
> —Les Brown

As a Million Dollar Speaker, you should now be clear on who you serve and the result you help them achieve. You settled that when you created your refined marketing statement in Chapter 4.

Mediocre speakers guess about what their audiences want. They hope for the best. Million Dollar Speakers research what their ideal clients believe is holding them back from achieving the results they desire. Million Dollar Speakers listen first and then build their presentation around what they hear.

By listening to your audience, you have already identified what they believe is the biggest obstacle holding them back.

Let's use what we do in our business as an example. We help speakers and entrepreneurs achieve 6- and 7-figure days through the events they host.

After finding out what the audience truly wants (in this case, to crush 6 figures in one day), the next step is asking them, "What's the biggest thing holding you back from doing a 6-figure day?"

They often say, "I don't have a big list. How will I sell enough tickets to have a 6-figure day?"

Whatever your business is, you want to know what's holding them back from achieving their goals. Don't blow past this important detail. Remember, this is about listening to your audience.

No matter the circumstance for what's holding them back, you have to ask yourself mentally: *Why do they believe this to be true?*

If you don't know the belief behind their reasoning, you cannot attack it.

What is it that they believe about their circumstance that is inhibiting them from achieving the result that they want?

Is that belief true or false?

If it's false, you've gotta break that belief and replace it with a new one.

The false belief in the above example is, "I need a big list to sell tickets to if I want to have a 6-figure day."

As the expert, you can identify your audience's false beliefs.

False beliefs keep your audience from achieving something because they *believe* they are incapable of achieving it. The problem isn't the situation they're in. The problem is their *false belief* about how to get out of the situation they're in. They cannot see the forest for the trees.

As a transformational speaker, your job is to rescue them from this self-imposed prison.

But you can't just tell them, "Your false belief isn't true!" That has a very low likelihood of persuading them away from their belief. If you tell them the opposite of what they believe, you're creating an opportunity for an argument.

You need them to experience the pain that comes with the belief they currently hold. And then you need them to experience the elation of *being freed* from that belief. They can then decide for themselves, based on their own mental journey, that the belief they hold is false.

When THEY come to the conclusion themselves, they believe it.

So, you need to ask yourself, "What can I say to help them experience the mental epiphany that will challenge and shift that belief?"

You could tell …

- a story from your personal life
- a client story

- a story from history
- a parable or metaphor

How are you going to do this? By using the bits framework.

How Are Bits Structured?

Have you ever listened to someone drone on and on about themselves? They tell their story, saying,

"Oh my gosh! My life is so hard. I was really struggling one day, and I tried to focus on my work. But then my neighbor came over, and I was like, I'm so stressed out. And so I told her about all the crazy stuff happening at work. And then I took a break and we went on a walk. And it was fun, I guess, but then I was still stressed. But I had to finish this project before I could go unwind ..."

They keep going, and they keep saying "I" or "me." It's all about them. Their thoughts, their feelings, their actions, their experiences.

Speakers tell stories because they've been told that "stories sell." And while this is true to an extent, many speakers spend a lot of time only talking about themselves. They never shift to their audience's perspective because no one ever taught them the framework that we're going to teach you.

This framework is all about how you communicate your bits. This framework is how you become a great speaker.

Great speakers *start* with the first person, "I," or, if they're telling a story about someone or something else, "he, she, or it." Then they quickly shift the point of view to the second person, "you."

It looks something like this:

"I was struggling financially, and I couldn't seem to catch a break. I took on a second job, but that burned me out. I tried applying to higher-paying jobs, but I didn't get a single interview. You know how when you try everything and nothing seems to work? You start thinking to yourself, *I'm just not good at this.* You feel like a failure, honestly. But then ... you change your mindset. All it takes is a subtle shift for you to regain your confidence."

Do you see how that started with an "I" statement and then quickly shifted to "you" being the focus? You've built a character in your story that is representative of each person in your audience. By shifting to the second person, they can see themselves in what you are saying.

It's a very simple and subtle shift but it's incredibly powerful.

Remember:

When you're telling a story, your purpose is not to tell *your* story. Your purpose is to tell them *their* story.

Why? Because you want them to *feel* it.

So how do you make them *feel anything*? You shift from your perspective to theirs as quickly as possible. You invite the reader to imagine that they are a part of the story. This sets the stage for the evolution of your bits.

Here's the basic framework:

- Start by telling a story, in first-person (I) or third-person (he/she/it)

- Shift to second-person (you)

- Share your important point

- Shift to a perceived enemy in third-person (they)

- Wrap up with a powerful soundbite

BIT STRUCTURE

See if you can spot the shifts in this story from Eileen's book, *One Day Cash Machine*™:

> I read a story in a crazy-good book called *You²* about a fly that was stuck behind a window.
>
> It was a flurry of frantic, frenetic energy, desperately fighting against the windowpane, struggling to get outside. It wanted to be free, and it was trying *everything* ...

While ten feet away, with just a few seconds of flight—an open door was awaiting the fly, leading to unrivaled freedom.

I wonder, how many times do you find yourself thinking that working harder equals wealth? Or thinking, *If I just do all the right things, earning it through years of effort ...*

I'll finally hit $1M? or $20M? or $1B?

But *what if* wealth didn't come from *more* effort, more energy, more long hours ... but wealth came from a few short moves?

Moves of sudden grace.

Too often, we think in terms of incremental growth. Slow addition. Putting in the hard yards to get the ball down the field.

Experts like to say, "You gotta hustle!" They preach you need a hit podcast, a YouTube channel that has 9 million subscribers, an Instagram account with a blue check ...

But what if you didn't?

Did you catch the shifts?

Start with a first-person story: *I read a story in a crazy-good book ... about a fly ... it was a flurry of frantic, frenetic energy ...*

Shift #1 to second person: *How many times do you find yourself thinking ...*

Make the point: *What if **wealth came from a few short moves** ...*

Shift #2 to a third-person perceived enemy: *Experts like to say ... **they** preach you need a hit podcast ...*

Once you see it, you'll never be able to unsee it. If you listen to great speakers, you'll start to hear it in all their speeches.

You will also notice when speakers are spending too long in the "I" part of the story, and not pivoting to "you." You will see the audience's eyes glazing over, heads starting to droop, and the speaker losing the room.

But that won't be you. Because you know how to build a framework that not only keeps your audience engaged but actually *moves them* to a new way of thinking. You'll have the crowd on their feet cheering in loud applause in no time.

Let's break this down bit by bit (pun intended) to illustrate an example of this framework in action.

SECTION II: THE SYSTEM

Introduce the I/He/She/It Struggle

Start with the subject and describe their current circumstances. This can be from your perspective (I) or someone else's (he/she/it). Introduce your struggle or a third-person metaphor for the struggle you're trying to overcome.

> I had a client named Jon. Jon was a very smart and capable guy who worked as a pastor. He loved his work, but he felt called to do something beyond the walls of his church.
>
> However, he had a big problem. He didn't want to use his role or authority as a pastor as a means to sell a product or service.
>
> Most of his social media following consisted of his local church parishioners, so he was unwilling to market or advertise or sell in any way to his existing following on social media. And he didn't have an email list.

You've introduced the character's struggles. Now you want to share the character's feelings.

> Jon was frustrated. He felt this desire to help in a different context but didn't feel like he had the resources or access to resources to make the vision in his heart a reality.

Once you've established the character's story, it's time to shift the point of view.

Shift to "You" Struggle

Now you're going to share Jon's feelings with the audience in the second person to get them fully engaged. Sharing his feelings from the "you" perspective gives them the chance to experience the story as if they are in Jon's shoes.

This is now *their* experience.

> You know what it feels like when you have a desire to do something big, but you feel like you don't have what you need to get the job done?

So you start looking around at what other people are doing ... Everywhere you look, they're doing something that you can't do because they have something you don't have.

Anybody know that frustration?

And when you get to this place where you don't trust that you have what you need to get the job done, you feel powerless and frustrated.

Now, the audience can fill in the blanks of this frustration with their own situation, which sets you up perfectly to hit the peak of your presentation.

Present the Point

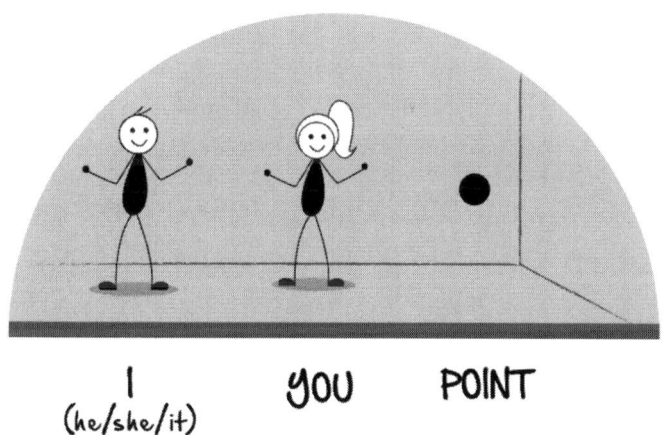

After introducing the first person struggle and shifting to second person to instill it in their minds, the audience is primed and ready. You can now tell them what they need to hear.

That's how Jon was when he came to me—defeated.

He said, "I don't have a list. I don't have a list *at all*. I can't sell tickets to an event."

I replied, "Jon, you don't need a list. You can just use someone else's list."

Did you catch the point? The first-person character said it. When presenting the point, there will be objections in the audience's minds. The next step is to let the audience experience them from Jon's perspective.

Jon opened his mouth, prepared to respond, and then stopped. He cocked his head to the side and said, "What do you mean, 'use someone else's'?"

"Jon, have you ever bought tickets to a movie?"

"Yeah," he said.

"Cool! Where'd ya hear about it?"

"I saw one of the actors promoting it on a late-night TV show," he said.

"Did that actor or movie company own that TV show?"

"No."

"So you're telling me that the movie companies promote their movies to audiences and channels that they don't own?" I said this with an air of incredulity and mock dismay.

He shot back, "Yeah, but I can't get on one of those shows!"

"Have you ever been to an online event like the one you want to run?" I asked.

"Sure," he said.

"Awesome! How did you hear about it?"

"I was listening to a podcast," he said. A wave of realization swept over his face. "The event promoter and speaker were being interviewed …" His voice trailed off, knowing the truth bomb I was about to drop as his coach.

"OOOOHHHHHH!" I said. "So you're telling me that this guy runs an event like the one you wanna run, and he was able to promote his event to SOMEONE ELSE's podcast listeners?!"

At this point, you want to engage your audience. If you're in a Zoom room or on Facebook live, ask those watching to engage in the chat. If you're hosting a live event, get the audience screaming and cheering and shouting out a response.

Hold on … Guys … Let me just poll the audience real quick! In the chat, guys, do you need a big list to sell tickets to your event? Yes or no? Put it in the chat!

Chris says no. Suzy says no. Brian says no. Donny says no. Lots of "no's" coming in. Everybody gets it!

You don't need to have a big list! You just need to sell to somebody else's list.

And that's exactly what Jon did. Jon ended up selling hundreds of tickets to his event after promoting it on two easy podcast interviews. He made over one million dollars at that event.

And that is how you present your point. That is how you get your audience EXCITED about how they can eliminate their false belief. *That* is how easy it is to find a solution to their problem.

Next, we're going to teach you how to make them *feel*. Otherwise, they won't *do* anything. (Well, except maybe take a nap during your presentation!)

Enter the perceived enemy.

Introduce "They" (the Perceived Enemy)

Your audience needs to get angry about the fact that they didn't believe this idea before—that they've been held captive by these false beliefs. They've been held back from their God-given freedom and ability, imprisoned by invisible chains of thought.

> And this is what happens in your mind when you're constantly bombarded by the thinking and beliefs of people who are trying to sell you something. They make it seem harder than it is. They make you think you need to do *everything*.
>
> Eventually, the bombardment becomes so incessant that you start believing them!
>
> The Facebook ads consultants are telling you that you need to run Facebook ads. The YouTube ad experts are telling you you need to be running paid YouTube ads.
>
> The organic marketers and the gurus are telling you to post everywhere all the time. "Post 5-7 times a day," they say! Why? "Well, you've gotta grow your list and your following!"
>
> And if you listen to them, you'll find yourself posting 957 times a day and trying to build an email growth list and trying to run Facebook ads and trying to run YouTube ads and trying to grow your following ...
>
> Have you ever just felt tired trying to obey the noise of what you're "supposed" to do?
>
> Well, I've got a message for every guru ... I've got a message for every ad agency trying to sell you their

services ... I've got a message for every coach and consultant trying to tell you what you need to do ...

Here it is ... Are you ready?

You're jazzing up your audience. You're getting them even more excited. They're angry at the perceived enemy, and they want to know what's next.

Excite Them with a Soundbite

This last part is what makes your audience think that you are an *amazing* speaker.

A soundbite is a technique used by great speakers, and if you choose to incorporate them, watch out, because your audience will be blown away!

The definition of a soundbite is "a brief catchy comment or saying."

A friend of Eileen's, Richie Norton, calls them "tweetable repeatables."

It's like "ear candy" for your audience.

If you've ever listened to a great speaker, you'll notice that they'll tell an engaging story, make their point, and then punctuate it with a "one-liner."

That one-liner is their soundbite. It makes the crowd go, "Oooh!" or "Whoa!"

The most powerful soundbites have some form of alliteration, rhyme, or contrast.

Some soundbites Eileen has become known for are:

Do it NOW!

Procrastination is the assassination of your destination.

Immersion causes conversion.

A powerful soundbite truly lands the point in the mind of the listener. And it's often a line they'll repeat back later—when making the investment into your program.

The new client will say something like "I just have to do it NOW!"

Let's get back to the end of the Jon example. You've taken them through each step of the bit framework, and now you're ready for the soundbite.

> My message for every guru telling you what you need is this ...
>
> Plot twist! *You don't need a big list!*
>
> *You don't need a big list.*
>
> If you know that's right ... If you're saying to yourself or out loud, "Plot twist! *You don't need a big list!*" put "plot twist" in the chat!
>
> Some of you thought I came here to give you more stuff to do.
>
> But would it be OK if I instead make your life more simple so you can get better results?
>
> *You don't need a big list!*
>
> If that makes sense, say "yes" in the chat. Type it in right now so I know that you understand that *you don't need a big list.* You can just sell to someone else's.
>
> Now, how many of you would like to know how to easily get someone else to sell your event tickets to their list? Type in the chat, "me!"

At this point, your audience will be clamoring to work with you. They'll be repeating this statement like crazy after the event to solidify their newfound belief and identity.

Stack Your Soundbites

Want an advanced move? You can do one soundbite or **a soundbite stack**.

After you tell your story using the bits framework, you might share a quote from a credible authority (your first soundbite in the stack). Follow that one with another powerful quote (your second soundbite in the stack). And then, once you've anchored to two higher authorities, create your *own* quote.

When you precede your original quote with two quotes from well-respected, known authorities, their credibility gets transferred to you. This is what's called "borrowed ethos." As you stack each quote, you're building momentum. To the audience, it will feel like a rising crescendo, resulting in a mic-drop moment for you.

Here's an example from Eileen's *One Day Cash Machine*™ book:

> W. Clement Stone understood that the number one enemy you and I have to overcome as entrepreneurs is this:
>
> Procrastination.
>
> He understood that the greatest enemy of wealth isn't a mindset issue. It isn't wealth or resources. It isn't upbringing or circumstances.
>
> It's delay.
>
> I love this quote by Napoleon Hill: "Successful people make decisions quickly and change them very slowly. Unsuccessful people make decisions very slowly and change them often and quickly."
>
> And in the words of Michael Hyatt, "Excessive planning is just a fancy way to procrastinate."
>
> I like to say it like this:
>
> Procrastination is the assassination of your destination.

Note the anchoring to authorities like W. Clement Stone, Napoleon Hill, and Michael Hyatt. Can you feel the borrowed ethos?

Use quotes from people you admire. Stack one after the other. For your original soundbite, take your time to craft something memorable. Use rhyme, alliteration, or contrast. Make it musical.

Stack your final soundbite and watch the crowd go WILD.

It's Okay to Reorganize Your Bit

As you get more comfortable, you'll learn that you don't have to follow this exact sequence every single time. Some speakers make their point using a soundbite. Some speakers will start the story with "they" and move the audience immediately into the emotion caused by a common enemy.

Sometimes, when telling a longer story, a speaker will shift from "I" to "you" and then bring the reader back to the story by reintroducing the "I."

Typically in longer speeches or longer stories inside of a speech, there is a back-and-forth dance between the "I" and the "you." In this way, you bring the audience into the larger story and then take them back out into their own feelings.

You're painting such a vivid and realistic picture that the audience member forgets that they're listening to a speaker. They're completely immersed in the story.

This framework has a very clear and simple flow.

But remember that speaking is an art. Once you have mastered all the elements, you can reorganize your bits in ways that excite an audience and ignite their emotions.

Have fun with it!

"Storytelling is the most powerful way to put ideas into the world today."

—Robert McKee

13

TAKE YOUR SPEAKER BIT TECHNIQUES TO THE NEXT LEVEL

> "If you have an important point to make, don't try to be subtle or clever. Use a pile driver. Hit the point once. Then come back and hit it again. Then hit it a third time."
>
> —Sir Winston Churchill

When I was growing up, I remember a particularly charismatic preacher who was always invited to the largest conferences and celebrated as one of the most profound and powerful speakers.

Pastor Mooney didn't speak like everyone else.

I couldn't put my finger on it, but he had a more circular approach to speaking … as opposed to linear. Other speakers were monotone and even mono-directional with their speaking. Pastor Mooney was constantly changing his tone and pace.

It made everything feel more interesting.

It felt more creative—more compelling.

And judging by the crowd response, the audience felt it too.

From my beginner's point of view, it looked like chaos and disconnection that suddenly came together almost magically.

It was as if Pastor Mooney was Mickey Mouse in *Fantasia*. A grand conductor, bringing to life a symphony that came together in a resounding climax of power and persuasion.

For many years, it was a mystery how Pastor Mooney was able to conduct this experience so consistently with message after message, week after week at his church.

It wasn't until I heard him explain how he thought about presenting his messages that I realized he was executing what Eileen and I now call a "bit barrage."

Once I could see how the magician was moving his hands, I started to see the pattern among some of the world's other more unique and celebrated speakers.

It is advanced.

I'm going to attempt to present it in its simplest form.

A single bit is a linear approach to speaking, but a bit barrage aims directly at the target of false belief and hits the bull's-eye, taking it out.

Understand that just as a single bit can be sequenced differently, so can a bit barrage.

Since a bit barrage involves multiple bits, this multiplication on multiplication leads to an exponential number of differences.

Activate the Bit Barrage

Mediocre speakers, when they have a point to make, say it only once. If you listen to presentations, YouTube videos, podcasts, webinars, or live videos, you'll notice that most speakers take this approach.

They'll tell a story, get to their point, and then it's like, "Boom! I said it! Done!" That's as far as it goes. End of presentation. Party's over. Everyone can go home.

But Million Dollar Speakers, who are masters at creating emotion around their message, don't just say it once. They share multiple, distinct stories that all drive home the *same* point. Think of it, again, like shooting arrows at a target. Great speakers don't just shoot one arrow and call it "done." They shoot multiple arrows at the same target, completely obliterating the false belief holding their audience captive.

There's a *single* point your entire audience must believe to *become* who they want to be.

One speaker bit may or may not connect and resonate, which is why we usually recommend at least four bits. For example, if you use a sports metaphor, you're not going to connect with those who aren't sports fans. And if your examples center around parenting, you won't connect as well with those who don't have children. That's why you need multiple bits to drive home your main point.

Why do you need so many arrows targeting that one false belief? Well, let's imagine for a moment that your child was suddenly abducted. Would you send one person to try to find him or her? Or would you want as many trained professionals as possible working to bring back your baby? This example may seem a bit extreme, but it's how the greatest speakers in the world treat the weight of their messages.

Great speakers understand that their audience has been hijacked and enslaved by certain false beliefs, so they go after those invisible chains with full force. They barrage their audience with bit after bit until they've achieved the epiphany, the identity shift, and the declaration (more on declarations in a moment).

Each speaker bit in the bit barrage attacks the same point from a different direction (see the diagram below). No more pinning your hopes and dreams on a singular method. With this approach, you can really drive the point home. It's incredibly effective in its subtlety.

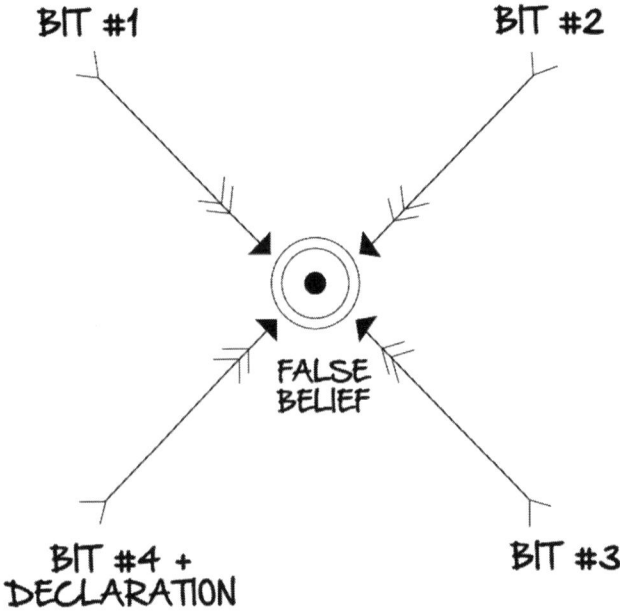

Every time you give a presentation, you'll tell not one, not two, but *three* bits that all lead to the same point. At the end of the three bits, believe it or not, you'll do *one more* bit. At the end of this fourth bit (which completes the X in the diagram), you will invite them to make a *declaration* of a new identity.

The number of bits per barrage is not scientific, but we've found that four is the average number of bits Million Dollar Speakers will tell to drive home the point.

Building Your Bit Barrage

Presenting a bit barrage works the same as presenting a single bit.

Let's start in the center.

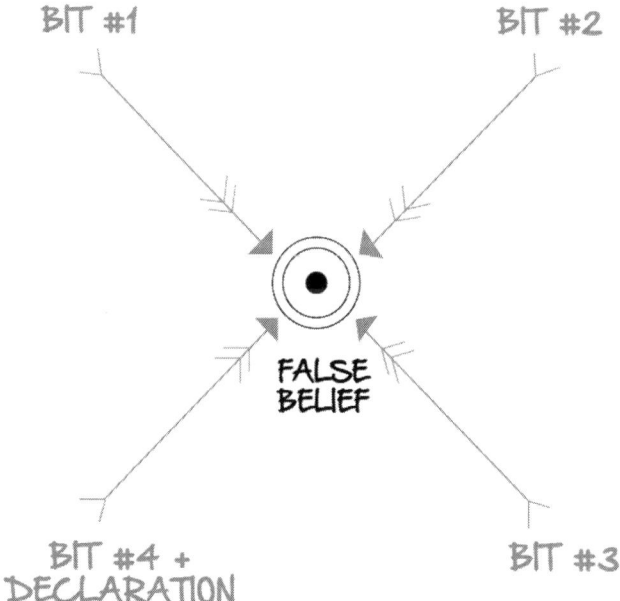

What's the false belief you want to obliterate on behalf of the individual in your audience?

You must be clear on this first. State it in a sentence.

False Belief:_____

What's the opposite of the false belief? What do you want them to believe? State it in a single sentence.

Stated belief:_____

Great, now what's the first story you want to tell, using the speaker framework, to attack this false belief? Write it down so you know it in an instant.

Speaker Bit #1

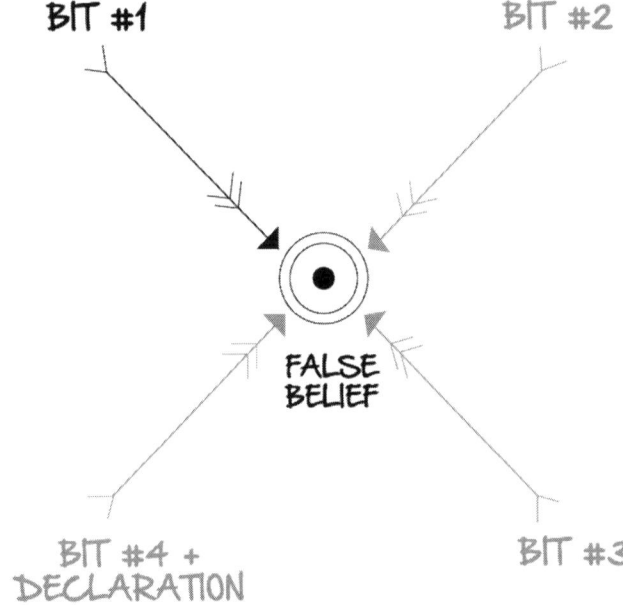

Story #1: _____

Now, using what you learned in the single bit chapter, let's get clear on the big components of that story using the bits framework.

I/He/She/It of the story:_____

Remember, when introducing a character, it helps to quickly describe the setting in which the character is now appearing. Paint a picture with words that appeal to multiple senses (sensory imagery). For example, "I was sitting at a bus station in Chicago. Icy December rain fell in a mud puddle of filth as I hunkered against the open plexiglass enclosure."

Shortly after you set the stage for your story, you'll want to present the conflict. Every good story has an element of surprise or drama. The conflict is what creates tension and triggers emotion in your audience. You'll want to know the specific conflict your main character is facing *before* you begin sharing your story. This conflict gives rise to the feelings the main character shares with the audience.

Next, you'll want to express the feelings of the main character in the story. Quickly shift to express those feelings in the second person "you." These feelings should be expressing the feelings of your audience, or at least a particular subset of your audience.

I often transition to the "feelings" with words like, "You know how when you … "

Feelings: _____

These feelings bring them into the story. You can stay in the pain of the struggle for a long time. Each audience member is taken on a journey of decision-making about the dilemma the character in the story is facing. It serves as a metaphor for a struggle that they are facing or may be facing.

Now, make your point. Make sure to state it clearly. This point is often spoken by a character in your story. Write your point here, saying it to the audience with conviction and clarity.

Point: _____

For example, your point may be, "You're stronger than you think you are." The false belief you want to overcome with this point is, "I don't think I can do this."

By making the point from a story they're immersed in, they now experience the truth of that point. It's not a debate. They're living it vicariously in the story.

They feel it. Remember that word? Make them FEEL it.

Now create a "they," either inside or outside the storyline, who will oppose or challenge your point.

Who is "they" in your story?

THEY: _____

You're the storyteller. Strike back against that fictional character in your story. Unite the audience against the lies of an enemy who does not believe! Have the "they" in the story share beliefs and doubts that may have been thought or believed by the audience before they heard this story.

Next, you need to generate a soundbite. In the energy of the moment, how are you going to make your point a tweetable repeatable?

Soundbite: _____

> A soundbite stack, which is an advanced move that is very effective when executed well, is best used sparingly. Having them in your speaking arsenal will elevate your presentations to new heights beyond your wildest imagination. However, you don't want to use a stack in every speaker bit because it will lose some of its power.

To design a soundbite stack, gather a couple of quotes from famous people that resonate and reinforce your point. Then, follow them up with your own soundbite.

Quote #1: _____

Quote #2: _____

Quote #3: But I say, _____

All three quotes, spoken back to back, will get the audience moving. I highly advise you to ask for a call-to-action along the way, getting them to say or type what you say. Remember, you want your audience to repeat your message back to you.

All of this—your story, characters, feelings, point, and soundbite—form Speaker Bit #1.

Let's work on your second speaker bit. We'll repeat the process with a new story and a different point.

Speaker Bit #2

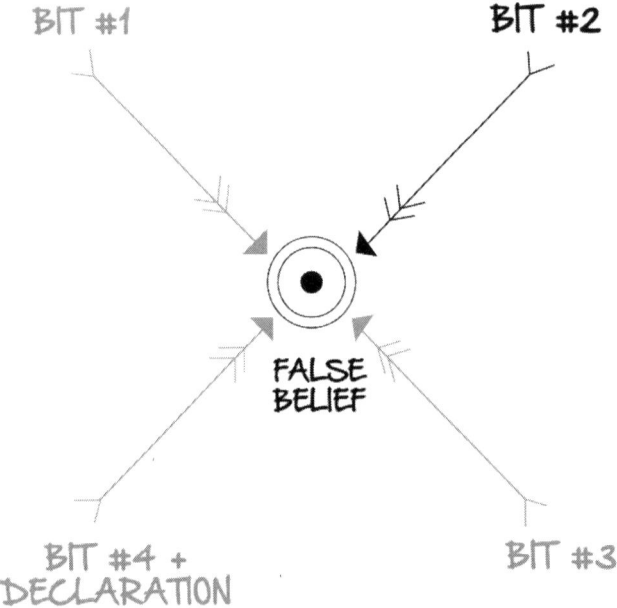

Speaker Bit #2 will need to be written just like Speaker Bit #1. This particular bit is another story with a different point that attacks the false belief from a different angle. This bit can be a story from history or place of inspiration and will attack your false belief with a new argument, thus bringing the audience to discard the false belief.

Speaker Bit #1 may have been a personal story that attacks the false belief with the point, "You're stronger than you think you are."

Speaker Bit #2 could be a motivational World War II story that makes a different point to intentionally dismantle the false belief. For example, a war story may prove a point such as, "Things that seem impossible are actually only uncomfortable." Notice, this is a different point to attack the same "I can't do this" false belief.

The goal is the same for each speaker bit in this bit barrage—to attack and overthrow the same false belief you identified in Speaker Bit #1.

Repeat the speaker bit process from the previous section with the content of Speaker Bit #2.

Speaker Bit #3

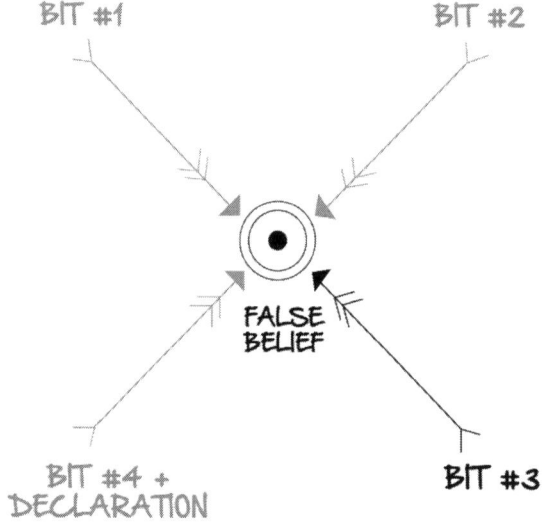

MILLION DOLLAR SPEAKER

Speaker Bit #3 is like #2, written from yet another angle of a person or group attacking the false belief. It can be designed from a story such as a book, sports, or a similar source of inspiration. The goal is to use an additional story from a different context that makes a point that demolishes the false belief.

The goal of each speaker bit in this bit barrage is the same—to attack and overthrow the false belief you identified in Speaker Bits #1 and #2.

Repeat the speaker bit process from the previous section with the content of Speaker Bit #3.

Do you see the repetition in these bits?

Speaker Bit #4 + Declaration

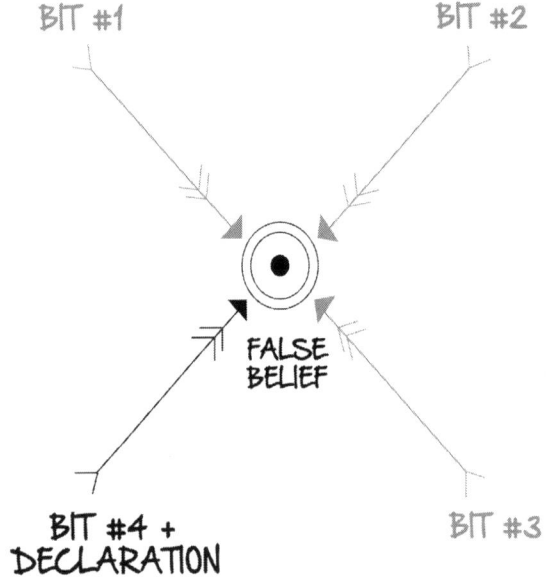

Speaker Bit #4 is often similar to the other three bits. The difference is that it ends with a declaration that is exactly the opposite of the false belief that you attacked throughout the bit barrage.

For example, let's assume the audience is struggling with the false belief, "I'm not capable."

You can then tell a story about a Mediocre Speaker who struggles to believe in her abilities. Contrast this false belief with a Million Dollar Speaker who believes that she is capable of greatness. It's the secret of the two identities in action!

In this final speaker bit, we'll position the Old Identity as the perceived enemy, and we'll ask the audience directly:

Now, declare which identity you want to be!

Do you wanna be a Mediocre Speaker ... or a Million Dollar Speaker?

They will ALL shout or type "Million Dollar Speaker!"

Then say:

If you wanna be a Million Dollar Speaker, say "I am ON FIRE!"

Say, "I can DO IT!"

I'll even raise my volume and contrast the two identities a few times. I really ramp up the audience at this point.

I may say:

A Mediocre Speaker says, "I can't do it."

But a Million Dollar Speaker says, "I can do anything."

A Mediocre Speaker says, "My boss won't let me."

But a Million Dollar Speaker says, "My boss can't stop me!"

A Mediocre Speaker says, "I give up."

But a Million Dollar Speaker says, "I'm just getting started!"

Can you feel the energy shift?

They will tend to think you're amazing after this process, but what's truly amazing is getting the audience to unleash *their* energy.

Now, you're going to add one final piece to really get the audience fired up: a declaration.

So at the end of Bit #4, my goal (and this one's a little advanced) is to get them to say, "I am a _____."

DECLARATION

They will DECLARE A NEW IDENTITY right then and there.

Are there any Million Dollar Speakers in the house? If you know that it's time for you to step up to your full potential, shout "I got this!"

Say it again: "I GOT THIS!"

Yeah, you do! Give yourselves a big round of applause.

Now, place your hand on your heart and say, "I am a Million Dollar Speaker."

Remember, people believe only 3% of what you say and 97% of what they say. That's why it's important to activate your audience to *say* what they believe.

If you get them to say it, they will believe it.

Can you imagine hearing a crowd all together declaring, "I am a _____!"

"I am a MILLION DOLLAR SPEAKER!"

You get to watch beliefs shift and identities transform right in front of you.

When you can move a room like that, congratulations! You have unlocked one of the greatest secrets of the world's most transformational speakers.

Now, don't think this is where your presentation ends. Million Dollar Speakers always end with an invitation.

Want to see us breaking down some of the best speeches ever? Go to this link, and we'll show you some live play-by-play analysis of great speaking:

MDSbonuses.com

14

DON'T HARM YOUR AUDIENCE, LEAD THEM

> "If you're not taking care of your customers, your competitor will."
>
> —*Bob Hooey*

Craig had completely knocked the ball out of the park.

The emotion I experienced while he was speaking was palpable. He shifted me and everyone watching could feel it.

It was a thing of beauty.

He had done what we trained him to do. He had captivated the audience with his speech. The response from the crowd told all the story that needed to be told.

They loved it.

I didn't want it to end, but I could feel the close coming.

Declaration. He hit it like an old pro. They were shouting their new identity at the stage.

"I am a ____! I AM A ____!"

He had shifted them. Identities followed epiphanies in a masterful stacking of stories, culminating in a raucous declaration from the audience. They were shouting their newfound identities, full of new beliefs that would lead them to the obvious next decision to go all-in on investing in themselves.

And then, at this high point of emotion, with everyone wanting more, Craig said something that made my heart sink into my stomach: "Thank you, ladies and gentlemen! Goodnight!"

He walked off stage as the audience applauded with glee.

What?! No, I thought to myself. How could this happen? Those poor people! I jumped on my phone to text Craig.

"Craig!!! That was INSANE!" I texted. "Great job! Super proud of you. Let's tag in tomorrow to review, okay?"

"Sure thing," he said.

The next day I jumped on a Zoom to meet with Craig. After congratulating him on his epic impact on the crowd, I gently shifted the conversation. I wanted to alert him that his speaking was accidentally having a disastrous effect on both his audience and on his ability to get his powerful message out in a bigger way.

"Craig, there is one part of the speech that I want to discuss with you to help you grow this thing to the next level."

"Okay," he said. "Shoot."

"Why did you end after the declaration? It was like a rock concert in there."

"Well, I remember you saying to leave them wanting more," Craig shared. "They were at a high point and it felt right."

"No doubt," I said. "They were asking for an encore, so I'm sure they have good feelings about everything you represent and will be searching you out. Now, I already know the answer to this question, but I'm going to ask it this way to help you learn a valuable lesson right now. I want this to stick, so do I have permission to really coach you here?"

"Yes, please," he said.

"Okay, here's my question: Do you want APPLAUSE or do you want REAL IMPACT?"

He cocked his head sideways at me a little, clearly taken aback by the question. "Well, real impact. You know that, Joe."

"I do," I replied gently, "but I need to be very direct, Craig. It's important that you hear me if you're gonna have the impact you want to make.

"You missed a real opportunity to help a lot of people. Thankfully, the damage is not irreversible. But you did all that hard work to take them to a place where you could help, and then you abandoned them. Right at the moment of their greatest opportunity to truly become.

"This was not your intention. I know your heart. But nevertheless, it was the outcome. Maybe I can say it this way ... there's a difference between an influencer and a leader. Influencers are focused on the applause of the crowd. But leaders—Million Dollar Speakers, like I'm teaching you to be—are focused on what's of best service to the audience.

"There's nothing wrong with the applause. It's an important aspect of getting them excited and going all-in on becoming who God is calling them to be. But, and this is a big but: applause is a tool, not the goal.

"The goal is transformation."

Craig jumped in, clearly troubled by the directness of my approach. This guy cared, and the last thing he wanted to hear is that he had somehow missed an opportunity to serve his clients at the highest level.

"Joe, they *were* transformed. You could see the light bulbs going off in their brains. They were overjoyed and shouting their newfound declarations of identity. I mean, I ran the play. It was awesome. Help me … what did I do wrong? I don't understand."

"I know you care about your audience," I said, "so that's why I'm delivering this message to you this way. Because the world has a different message than the one I'm about to deliver to you."

This is what I shared with Craig, almost word for word:

"You effectively served them with excellence to help them understand that they should be all-in on becoming the version of themselves that you so eloquently presented. But at the height of emotion, when they were ready to COMMIT to that new identity, you left them standing at the altar like a runaway bride leaves a groom.

"Mediocre speakers measure their message's effectiveness based on applause. But Million Dollar Speakers measure their effectiveness based on leadership.

"Leaders offer an opportunity to take the next step with them.

"Yes, leave them wanting more, but then show them how to *get more!* How to take the next step to experience more transformation with you.

"Yes, transformation happened in that room last night, no doubt. But, as you well know, the reality of the world is going to push back and challenge this newfound commitment they declared. And you've left them alone to try and fight that on their own.

"There's a saying that the old pros used to say, 'You cannot learn to ride a bike at a seminar.'

"Inspiring people isn't enough. Teaching people isn't enough. They need leadership and support. They need a clear path for committing to the next steps.

"There is so much coming at them. We cannot expect them to carry this newfound transformation alone.

"Call them to action. Invite them to take the next step with you. Always invite them to take the next step.

"Million Dollar Speakers do not leave people hanging to fend for themselves.

"Million Dollar Speakers invite them to become, show them the path, and then invite them to the next step.

"If there is no invitation to work with you at the end of your presentation, you have not done your job."

I could see the realization dawn on Craig's face as he sat back in his seat, but he remained silent. I felt bad that I had knocked the wind out of his sails because his speech absolutely crushed, but I knew this valuable lesson would serve him for decades if he could really feel the weight of it.

After a big sigh, Craig finally said, "You know ... there's this feeling in society that if you're trying to help someone but there's any sort of business attached to it, it's somehow less authentic.

"I think I kinda bought that a little last night. I wanted to help them. But, now I'm asking myself ... did I?

"Yeah, I helped them a little. Hopefully, the transformation will stick. But what would really be in THEIR best interest?

"What would *really* be in their best interest would be to get more support in becoming what they've now committed to.

"What would really be in their best interest is for me to have an entire infrastructure of support that will serve them in becoming and achieving what they've now committed to.

"But that has taken a massive investment on my part to build the team and infrastructure necessary to do that on their behalf.

"I cannot keep the infrastructure in place without money. I'm torn."

"Craig, I understand the money issue ... sometimes early in a business, it's a good exercise to check yourself to see if what you're selling is good for humanity. That's healthy and ethical.

"Let me ask you this, which service option will help them more?

"Option 1: You try and do it all for free in your free time while you work to take care of your family another way.

"Option 2: You take on the financial risk and challenges to create something awesome knowing that it's going to create infrastructure that serves your clients at the highest level.

"Leaving their money out of the equation, which serves them better?" I asked.

"Obviously, building out an infrastructure that gets 100% of my attention and possibly some additional team and infrastructure to serve them," Craig said.

"Okay," I said.

"So, we've agreed that the highest form of service is to build something, aka a business or program, that serves them and helps them to achieve their desired result instead of you trying to part-time it for free, yes?"

"Yes," Craig said.

"Craig, you're doing a great job speaking. You crushed it. But, if you're ready to take your clients to the next level, would it be okay if I showed you how Million Dollar Speakers do this while making significantly more money?"

"Of course," he said.

"Okay, I'm going to show you how Million Dollar Speakers decide what to offer their audience to go deeper with them," I said.

Craig leaned in, anticipating the big reveal of how to lead his audience into even deeper, more lasting transformation. What I shared with him, Eileen will share with you in the next chapter.

15

POSITIONING YOURSELF TO MAKE AN INVITATION WITHOUT SOUNDING SALESY — FROM EILEEN

"Stop selling. Start helping."

—Zig Ziglar

The apartment was eerily quiet. The fluorescent ring light was radiating with such an intense heat it felt like I was an active suspect of interrogation. I was alone. Just me, my laptop, and a floodlight of misery.

The Zoom attendees would be coming in soon, and I would be speaking and making an offer at the end. The idea of asking people for money sent shivers of terror down my spine.

Will they get offended if I sell them something?

What if they get angry and say something negative?

Will they get value from what I'm selling?

What am I even doing?

I thought I was going to be sick.

Harrison, my husband, was kind enough to take our three kids out of our small apartment to the park, so the house would be quiet. He was being so supportive, even though we hadn't seen a financial breakthrough yet.

As I steeled my nerves and reminded myself of some powerful sales principles I had been learning, an inkling of a new thought came into my mind. *Maybe this is it*, I thought. *Maybe tonight is the night I will begin making money as a speaker.*

My First Invitation

At the end of my message, I took a long, deep breath. And began my invitation to apply:

> If you'd like to dive deeper into Getting Unstuck & Discovering Your Purpose, I have a special invitation for you! It might not be right for all of you, and that's okay, but it might be perfect for those of you who'd like someone to take you by the hand and help you discover more about your unique skills, talents, and gifts ...

What happened next still surprises me to this day. The notifications in my call calendar went off. *Ding. Ding. Ding.* In the new window I had open, appointments started appearing on my calendar.

Omg! They do want to go deeper!

Divorce Yourself from the Outcome

To put yourself in the best possible posture to sell anything, divorce yourself from the outcome. Meaning: stay disconnected from the *need* for anybody to do *anything*. For them to...

- Like your speech
- Comment on your video
- Respond to your presentation
- Buy your service or product

When you don't need anybody to clap for you, respond to you, or give you money, you're in a powerful position. It enables you to be able to help, not sell. I like to call it "staying leaned out."

Stay Leaned Out

Did you ever have a crush on somebody in high school, and part of the attraction was that they were "hard to get?"

As a sophomore, I had a near-obsessive crush on a senior boy. Sigh. He was the epitome of cool. His aloofness had all the girls magically drawn toward him.

It was as if he was reading a hidden guidebook on how to attract females. Whatever he was doing, it was working. I'd strategically position myself by my locker and glance at him as he walked by. He'd nod slightly and keep going. I would lose my mind. *He noticed me!*

Why did his inattention make me like him *more?*

Yet when a fellow classmate would sit down next to me at lunch, attentive and kind, needy for my attention, all I wanted to do was leave. Here's the principle:

"Needy energy" pushes people away.

"Leaned out" energy attracts others toward you.

Stop Needing the Sale

Have you ever watched a speaker get nervous when they start talking about price? It happens all the time. This is especially true when they're about to say a high price or a price they've never said before.

One of the keys to remaining calm and confident when you get ready to talk about the price of your offer is to recognize that your audience wants you to succeed. When you're speaking, you're conveying emotion, and the audience will mirror that emotion. If you're feeling weird and nervous, guess how they're feeling? Weird and nervous!

One of the things that will sabotage your sales is needing the sale. Your "needy energy" for needing somebody to do anything—to respond, to type in the chat, or to comment—is sabotaging the sale.

Instead, the energy that you want to have during the part where you share your offer is:

"Buy or don't buy. I don't need your money."

Now you may say to me, "Well, my bank account looks like *it* needs money." Maybe you need sales, maybe you need money, but you don't need *that* sale. You don't need it so badly that you come across as desperate.

Before your invitation to the audience to work with you, say something like this:

> *You can buy or not buy. I know my products are good and will help you. I know they will help you get the result you are looking for more quickly. I'm going to invite you to take the next step, but if it's not the right time for you, that's okay. I don't need you to do anything.*

Stay cool, calm, and collected. Being needy will have the opposite effect that you want on your audience.

I was once the victim of a time-share presentation. The salesman wanted us to buy so badly, the atmosphere almost felt threatening. Everything screamed: "Buy this or else." The level of pushiness was stifling. All I wanted to do was run away. My husband and I narrowly escaped with our lives, but needless to say, the salesman's neediness evaporated *all* attraction to the sale.

Have you ever experienced this? Walking past one of those kiosks at the mall? Casually browsing at a used car lot? I'll bet those pushy environments also make you want to run away.

Don't let this valuable lesson of how *not* to do sales go to waste. Here's the lesson:

Your neediness will cause their speediness to the door.

In contrast, being "leaned out" means being 100% detached from *needing* the sale. When you put off a vibe that you don't *need* your audience to do anything, you'll feel less pressure. Let them know that you're here to help, and that's it.

When you're divorced from the outcome, you will feel free to:

- publish and go live on video
- get your message out
- offer your free resources
- sell your course
- invite them to your high-end program

Why?

Because you are just here to serve. You are here to help people. And that feels amazing!

And because of your chill, helpful vibe, a line of hungry buyers will be ready to purchase your best programs at your highest prices.

All you need now are enticing invitations to get your audience interested.

Three Kinds of Invitations Every Speaker Must Have

Different speaking environments allow for different invitations. Having these three offers ready will enable you to be the most prepared in any scenario.

Free Resource

Known online as a "lead magnet," this is a free digital product that is easily given to those who listen to your presentation. You could offer a video series, a checklist, a quiz, a PDF, or any number of free resources in exchange for the audience member's email address.

This enables you to market other paid products later to the people who opt in. We've seen it work best by putting a link, QR code, or "Text this number!" on a public screen, which people can easily visit to opt in for the free resource.

Many speaking venues won't allow you to sell at the event, so it's best to have a free resource ready. Having a free giveaway will equip you to take advantage of the opportunity to gather email addresses and contact information for later marketing.

Low-Ticket Products

In environments where you are allowed to sell something, having a lower-priced product is a wonderful way to monetize your speaking. This could be on your social media, at a guest-speaking opportunity, or in an interview on a podcast or YouTube show.

Having a book, course, or event ticket to sell helps you not only continue the conversation with your listeners but also opens the door to creating a beautiful relationship with them.

Out of all the options, we'd recommend selling an event ticket. You can sell tickets at a price point such as $47 or $97 for people to attend your upcoming event. This option will provide the most accelerated path for listeners to grow, discover, and experience massive results.

High-Ticket Offers

Some environments will allow you to offer a high-ticket program or service. Typically, this would be your own hosted speaking event, or an event hosted by a partner or friend where you've been given permission to sell.

Premium products are often coaching packages, mastermind events, done-for-you services, or other higher-priced events. While you can make this invitation from the stage, going into the full offer with the price requires more advanced skills to keep the conversion metrics high.

As a guideline, anything over $2,000 is generally sold over the phone *after* the event. What this often looks like is inviting audience listeners to fill out an application. This "Application Invitation" is what we call the "No-Pitch Pitch." After the event is over, anyone who wants to go deeper will book a call with someone on your team, get their questions answered, and discuss payment options. It's the easiest way to close sales.

Cash Infusions

Out of the three invitations, making a high-ticket offer provides the biggest opportunity for a cash infusion. For example, let's say you have an offer for a group coaching program. The investment to join is $5,000. You talk to five people about your offer. The first four say no, and then you make your first sale with the fifth person. That person pays you $5,000 over the phone with their credit card.

Given those numbers, your "close rate" would be 20% (which is extremely low, so this example is considered a worst-case scenario). To keep that 20% close rate, you'd need 20 sales to make $100,000. That means you'd need to talk to 100 people.

Isn't that exciting? Would you be willing to talk to 100 people to generate six figures in sales? Or talk to 1,000 people to make 200 sales, resulting in a million dollars?

You're a *speaker*. Of course you would be thrilled to get sales like this!

This is why premium products are a great opportunity for speakers.

When I made my first invitation, a feeling of triumph began coursing through my veins. *I did it!* I was excited, not because they might buy something, but because I had the courage to make the offer.

I was proud that I had led my audience with confidence and left them wanting to work with me. When you start booking calls during your invitations, the same pride will wash over you. There's nothing quite like helping your audience to go deeper.

The next step is to ignite in them a burning desire that they can't quell without buying your irresistible offer.

16

THE HEAVEN AND HELL OF CREATING DESIRE

"Persuasion is often more effectual than force."

—Aesop

One day, several years ago, I was listening to a presentation by Russell Brunson. He was about to open the doors to his new event coming up called Funnel Hacking Live. I've since been to this event many times. I'm a mega-fan. It's the best event for marketers and entrepreneurs, like ever.

However, at the time, I had no intention of buying a ticket yet. I'm a last-minute sort of traveler. Many times I don't buy my airline tickets until the day before travel. Don't judge me. It's how I roll.

But then ... Russell said something during his pitch that made me NOT want to miss out. I *had* to get a ticket, and I had to get it *now*. I was so eager to grab my spot that I was scared I might not get in fast enough when he released the link. I did not want to miss this HUGE opportunity.

He created immense desire in his ticket sales pitch. So significant that I could barely focus I was so excited. Then, right when it came time to buy the ticket, I realized I didn't have my wallet. He released the link, and I panicked. I yelled to my wife, "Where's my wallet?!" She yelled back, "It's in the office!"

My wallet was in my office ... on the other side of the house. I was wearing socks, and my house is entirely tile floors. As I raced across the slippery tile to get my wallet and secure my ticket, I went sliding past the office doors as if my socks had become skis. Luckily, I stayed upright.

I scrambled back to the office doors I had just slid past, jumped into my leather office chair, and found my wallet. I quickly input my credit card and let out a big sigh of relief when the next page confirmed I had arrived on time with a note of "Congratulations!" I got my ticket.

This is what happens when you create desire for your audience. Screaming, yelling, mayhem, and possible bodily harm as your audience rushes to fulfill your directions.

Without desire, you'll be hard-pressed to elicit the kind of excitement and urgency I felt in getting that conference ticket.

As speakers, we often tell the audience what's amazing about the offer and say things like, "This is so good, you're really gonna love this." And we'll even create a vision for the future (called "future-pacing"), saying how awesome it is.

But future-pacing is not enough. You have to create a desire for the thing in order for them to be willing to give you money.

I learned this from entrepreneur and motivational speaker Dean Graziosi, and it has made me millions of dollars. Literally. It's insane. This is how I'd summarize it:

A big mistake most people make in their sales presentations is that they do not create desire.

Desire makes people want to sign up for your program before your event is even over. Desire is NOT to be underestimated.

Desire makes people wildly run through their houses looking for their wallets.

At the end of any presentation or event, once you've effectively used the bits framework, the audience will feel amazing. Since you're not a mediocre speaker who just settles for applause, you'll want to *invite* the audience to take the next step with you.

To create a deep level of desire in them to participate in the next step, all you need is a very simple framework, which I also learned from Dean Graziosi:

1. Describe a picture of hell without your offer.

2. Map out your offer.

3. Paint a picture of heaven with your offer.

From Hell to Heaven

Don't make the mistake of starting with heaven. What you don't want to do is start by saying, "I have this awesome offer. It's really, really great. It's called blah, blah, blah. Do you wanna hear about it?" Because your audience is going to be like, "Yeah, that's cool, but whatever."

Instead, you want to create *desire* so they're all screaming at you to tell them the offer. The way I do that is I first tell *their* story of hell *without my offer*.

I'll say something like:

"You guys know how when you're home alone and you're finally able to get some things done? You start working on something but get distracted because you don't know where to start. You're so frustrated and you think, *If someone could just come over and tell me what order to do this in, I could just be done with it and get it off my list!* Anybody been there before?"

So that's hell. I'll spend three to five minutes here, telling story after story. I'll even get silly or tell some stupid story, and it'll be humorous and make them laugh.

I'll tell hell upon hell. And it's all you, you, you, not we. Speakers often say, "We struggle with this and that, and we're blah, blah, blah …"

Get them to FEEL hell. **Say "YOU."**

So after I bring them to hell and tell the story of what they're experiencing without my offer, I'll then continue,

"And that's why we created this amazing [event/experience/destination] called [name of irresistible offer]. And at [name of the irresistible offer], once you get in there, you're gonna discover all the [heaven, heaven, heaven]."

Then I start creating a vision for what their life will look like after they experience this amazing offer. Once I spend a few minutes future-pacing them, I'll ask,

"How many of you want me to tell you about [name of irresistible offer]?"

But you've got to take them to hell first. Make them thirsty. If they're in the burning desert of hell, what do they want more than anything in the world?

Water!

Create hell without your offer, make them feel their desperate need for relief, then present your offer.

That's how you create desire.

17

THE THREE PRESENTATION FRAMEWORKS FOR YOUR IRRESISTIBLE INVITATIONS

"If you have a business and you're struggling financially, the solution is simple: Make more offers."

—Myron Golden

One of the biggest concerns many speakers have is that they're afraid they'll get to the invitation portion of their speech, get nervous, and say the wrong thing. They want to know the exact right words when they make their invitation.

When you make serving your audience the goal, inviting them to take the next step on the journey with you will become more normal and natural with practice.

As we've shared throughout the book, you want to make your audience feel like joining you *throughout* your presentation. After creating a powerful and emotional growth experience using speaker bits, the invitation is an obvious next step that many attendees will already want.

We recommend you use the heaven and hell principles to present your offer. And remember the invitation options from Chapter 15?

Each of the following frameworks aligns with either your free resource, low-priced product, or high-ticket offer.

Free Resource Invitation Framework

Setting:
This is typically done in the context of a speaking experience in which you are not the host or owner. Your free offer is great for guest speaking opportunities, podcast interviews, or links in your social media bio.

Transition Statement:
I know a lot of you guys are asking the question, What's next?

Hell Without:
Many times, listeners will come to an experience like this and feel excited and eager about going to implement what they've learned. And you know how when you go to implement things you learn and it's hard …

Tell a story about the hell they're almost guaranteed to go through as they try to implement what they've learned. Share the feelings of abysmal failure using the "I ➢ You" framework.

Offer:
Transition out of hell by saying something like,

Sometimes it's a struggle to [locate, assemble, research] all the _____ and it causes them to stay stuck, never accomplishing [end result]. So, I/our team assembled all that for you to save you all that time and money, for you to quickly be able to _____ . Would you find that helpful?

Heaven With:

When people download [Free Offer], you'll be able to [describe their result and feelings experienced and elation of heaven with that result].

Call to Action:

If you'd like to grab it, you can simply pull out your phone and text "I'm in" to (555) 111-2222 [or scan this QR code on the screen or go to this website] and you'll get a link to download [resource] 100% free.

Low-Ticket Product Framework

Setting:

This is typically done in the context of a speaking experience in which you are the owner. As long as you have express permission from the platform host, this low-ticket offer can also be done on podcast interviews, live social media interviews, or from the stage.

Transition Statement:

I know a lot of you guys are asking the question, What's next?

Hell Without:

Many times, listeners will come to an experience like this and feel excited and eager about going to implement what they've learned. And you know how when you go to implement things you learn and it's hard ...

Tell a story of hell of trying to implement what they've learned and share the feelings of abysmal failure using the "I ➤ You" framework. Feel free to throw in a client story of struggling alone, trying to implement, and failing. Or tell a story about anyone trying to implement anything and struggling.

Offer:

Transition out of hell by saying something like …

And the struggle so many people get stuck in ends up creating a vicious cycle that never allows them to grow into becoming the person that they want to be. That's why we created [Name of Low-Ticket Product].

Heaven With:

When people experience [Name of Low-Ticket Product], here's what happens.

First, [tell story of their result and feelings experienced and elation of heaven with that result].

Once that happens, [tell story of the next result and feelings experienced and elation of heaven with that result].

Then they tackle [tell story of achieving result and feelings experienced and elation of heaven with that result which came merely by buying the low-ticket offer].

And lastly we [tell story of the result and feelings experienced and elation of heaven with that result].

And then TADA! So, when you use our [Name of Low-Ticket Product], clients usually say, [tell story of the result and feelings experienced and elation of heaven with that ending result].

Anchor Price:

Now, to get our full training on the system that gets this result, it's typically [Pricing of Low-Ticket Product], but because [logical reason why it's significantly less here, e.g. they'll get it in book format or as a virtual course], we're offering a deal.

Investment:

You can get it today for just [tell them the significantly lower price]!

Call to Action:

Is that a good deal? If you think that this might be helpful for you, what I want you to do right now is to go to the following website.

Your website address or domain name needs to be so simple that when people hear it, they can type it out in three seconds. Don't get creative with your URL. If you're on a platform that will allow you to share your screen and walk them through step-by-step, it does help conversions. Often, this is not possible, so you can just explain it to them verbally.

Urgency:

You want to create a reason for people to act right now, if possible. For live events, you can create something that they're invited to in 10 minutes if they buy now. For example, you could offer to do a LIVE training explaining something they'd want immediately.

If the presentation is going to be evergreen, it may require scarcity of availability or immediate access to something else when they buy now.

You wanna get in there and buy right now because [give one of the reasons above for a reason why].

Bonus:

Have a BONUS available to push them over the top. This is advanced, but I'll often mention something that solves one of the audience's problems during my speech (we call this tactic a "token"). Then, when I do my bonus, I'll offer it free when they buy.

I'm actually going to do a super crazy deal just for you guys right here. When you buy right now I'm going to [tell them the BONUS or discount].

Or, if you use the token idea:

I'm actually going to do a super crazy deal just for you guys right here. When you buy right now, do you remember that thing I mentioned that helps you with X result, [name of thing]? When you buy right now, I'm also going to give you that for free.

Scarcity and urgency are your best friends in marketing. Try limiting availability to a certain number of people. For example, "There are only 12 slots available!" or "This offer is only good for the first 10 action-takers." You'll find that people will act a lot faster.

Call to Action:

Do a final call to action.

So, go to [name of website again] and get it right now.

The High-Ticket Offer Framework

The "Application Invitation" is also called the "No-Pitch Pitch."

This is the preferred pitch framework for people who've never sold from stage successfully and are selling something for more than $2,000. It's very soft and easy and does not require a significant amount of time.

> **PRO TIP:** Remember, before you use the "No-Pitch Pitch" script, the first thing you need to do is put yourself into a state of feeling amazing about your offer. You need to think your offer is a jewel that can't be turned down. This is so important! If you don't like your program, no one else will like your program. So, fall in love with your offer and put yourself in a state of loving your offer before you present!

Setting:

This is typically only done in the context of a speaking experience in which you are the owner. You wouldn't normally make an offer like this on someone else's podcast, show, or during some sort of interview, unless you have express permission from the platform host.

Transition Statement:

I know a lot of you guys are asking the question, "What's next?"

Reaffirm Identity:

How many of you are ALL IN on becoming like [Name of New Identity] and achieving [XYZ Result]? Give me an "ALL IN" in the chat if you're ALL IN.

I'll often really emphasize the contrast between being ALL IN versus someone who is not ALL IN. You want to get the audience self identifying as an all-in kind of person which correlates with all the beliefs of the New Identity.

Is it okay with you if I share a program we have to help you achieve [XYZ Result]?

Hell Without:

Many times clients will come to an event like this and feel excited and eager about going to implement what they've learned. And you know how when you go to implement things you learn and it's hard ...

Tell a story of the hell they would experience if they tried to implement everything they've learned all on their own. Using the "I ➤ You" framework, you could share about an unavoidable failure and the accompanying feelings of frustration, exasperation, and defeat. Just like you would for a low-ticket product, you could tell a story about anyone trying to implement anything and struggling.

Offer:

Transition out of hell by saying something like,

And the struggle so many people get stuck in ends up creating a vicious cycle that never allows them to grow into becoming the person that they want to be. That's why we created [Name of High-Ticket Offer].

Heaven With:

When people go ALL IN on being a part of [Name of High-Ticket Offer], here's what happens.

First we do [thing you do in your program] and once that's conquered, [tell story of the result and feelings experienced and elation of heaven with that result].

Once we've done that, next, clients do [next thing you do in process]—[tell story of the result and feelings experienced and elation of heaven with that result].

Then we tackle [tell story of achieving result and feelings experienced and elation of heaven with that result].

And lastly we [tell story of the result and feelings experienced and elation of heaven with that result].

And then TADA! Using our system [called ABC], clients usually say [tell story of the result and feelings experienced and elation of heaven with that ending result].

Permission:

I don't wanna do some big pitch—I want to jump back into the training real quick.

Because this isn't for everybody. However, there are some of you in here that this would be HUGE for you. There are good fits, and there are people who are NOT a good fit. For that reason, if you're interested in being a part, is it okay with you if I share how to apply to see if you're a good fit for this so that you can go ALL IN on yourself and we can help you work toward achieving [XYZ Result]?

Give me a big yes if that's ok.

Call to Action:

If you think that this might be helpful for you, what I want you to do right now is open up a new tab in your browser and go to the following website.

Fill out your application right there, and I want you to book a call RIGHT NOW. After you fill out your application, there will be a calendar where you can schedule a call with me or my team to talk through your application and answer any questions about how we can help you. Schedule your time to speak with us RIGHT NOW and we'll see you at the scheduled time to discuss.

Urgency:

We're going to go to a quick 10-minute break to let you complete your application right now. This offer that I just told you, I'm actually going to do a super crazy deal just for you guys right here, if you apply during the break!

It's ONLY going to be for people who apply and book a call during the break.

You may need time to talk to a partner or spouse, or may not have the time or money to take the next step, so you're not sure. Totally understandable. We may, as a company, be able to help with funding, and we know you have more questions about the investment, timing, etc. but that's the point of the call … to see if you're a good fit, and now is a good time.

SECTION II: THE SYSTEM

But, action takers rule, so ... now's your time to take action. We'll deal with any additional issues or questions on the call. Plus, there's a reward.

If we get on the call and you're a good fit, we're going to give you a Fast Action Event discount where you're going to get—

Add a bonus with a creative name or offer a special discount that they get for taking action now. For example, I might offer thousands of dollars off the retail price I normally charge or offer a bonus training that they want, etc.

So, if you think this may be for you, and you're serious—not just curious—and you want me to "take you by the hand into the promised land" ...

Then open up a tab right now and go to [your website], and fill out your application. Put your name in the box RIGHT NOW and get on our calendar.

We not only have a super cool deal, we also have access to a funding partner if you have decent credit.

I can't wait for me or someone on my team to strategize with you on how to [get this result/payoff].

Go to a break, end the session, or move into Q&A immediately after this invitation is made. The longer you are able to stay doing Q&A, the more applications will come in.

This is the invitation to apply. Don't sweat it! It's powerful and simple.

THE NEW WORLD OF 6- AND 7-FIGURE DAYS — FROM EILEEN

> "There is no strategic benefit to being the second cheapest in the marketplace, but there is for being the most expensive."
>
> —Dan Kennedy

At first, Kaci was completely resistant to the traditional form of high-ticket. She struggled with the stigma of it for years, associating it with thoughts like, *It's just about money. It's not about actually helping people with the tools they need to succeed.*

But in her own business, she was burning out, drowning, and in a constant state of stress, trying to figure things out. She started seeing how much she needed to be wildly cash flow positive to make the impact she wanted to make.

The minute she realized she could do a high-ticket offer her way—and serve people with incredible care—she held the vision that her company could be a refreshing option in the industry. She saw it wasn't about her anymore. She decided she needed to stand in the gap for others and help prevent them from investing in the wrong programs!

She was so nervous about making her offer to her first live event attendees. She frantically sent voice memos back and forth with me about her offer and upcoming workshop, and I said, "You know what you have here? You have a one-hour cash machine! Mine is one day, but yours is one hour!"

Kaci still didn't fully realize she had a $10,000 offer until she was literally looking her workshop attendees in the eyes. She realized then the impact it would have on their own vision for the future. It hit her like a bolt of lightning, and she was in complete shock. Her offer was powerful, unique, and absolutely valuable.

So many people said, "I'm in! Let's go!" She was feeling all the emotions … nervousness, excitement, but above all, bold clarity of mission with a commitment to serve.

Right out of the gate, five students signed up for her $10K program. She says that everyone who has come through her program has said, "Thank you for treating us like a human. Thank you for being there. This has completely changed my life and business." She is experiencing complete and utter joy.

That's the beautiful thing about premium offers—you have the time and the space to truly serve. You get to go deep with people.

Kaci says she spent years resisting making a high-ticket offer because of the label she had given it—what she didn't want it to be instead of realizing how powerful it could be. In her words, "It contains the power of redefining an industry."

What Lies on the Other Side of Resistance

Rasmus is a client in Denmark. He had a $5K offer when he came to us, and we were like, "Rasmus, you help build other people's businesses. What you have is a minimum $30K offer."

When we said that to him, he had so much resistance that he just left the call. We didn't know if we had gotten through to him since he didn't say much on the call. We found out later that he had actually gone back and listened to the recording of the call like ten more times. He made his team listen to it. He was trying to get himself and all of them to believe, "I have a $30K offer."

It was so cool.

So he thought about it. He just kept thinking about it, imagining it. And he said, "What if I do the same stuff I'm doing in my $5K offer inside of my $30K offer and I add some events? Something like mastermind events?"

Then he said, "What if I could do it in a super cool, amazing place? What if we did it at a castle?" And we were like, "That sounds awesome."

So he took the same program he had in his $5K offer, added a bunch of events, and then delivered the $30K offer in Castle Masterminds. Rasmus sold about 17 packages right out of the gate. *Seventeen* $30K packages. That is $510,000.

Shifting to Selling Is Serving

Another client, Kiana Danial, CEO of Invest Diva, used to HATE selling. She actually cried with me on the phone, saying, "I don't want to sell. I just don't want to do it!"

Then her paradigm completely shifted. She realized that selling is serving, selling is good, and selling is love!

She discovered that when you charge more, you get to SERVE people at a higher level. And it is a lot more fun, a lot more impactful. Now she *loves* hanging out with her high-ticket clients and says it's one of the greatest pleasures in her life.

She went from hating selling to hosting three virtual events in one calendar year, selling an incredible high-ticket offer. She made $640,000 at those events serving the people she loves.

My First 6-Figure Day

After my event in Houston, my business colleague Margot asked me how I managed to make $108,000 in a single day, with only eight potential buyers in the room.

That's a good question, isn't it?

I remember how exhausting it was to be on sales calls all day! And how I used to lie on my apartment floor, feeling like I was "listening myself to death" on the phone with people who didn't want to buy.

But that one event was like having a *super* fun sales call, by doing a *month's* worth of calls in one day.

Immersion Causes Conversion

When you're speaking to a group, it's as if the event becomes the sales call, and the immersion of the content converts your audience toward the sale the entire time.

At the end of the event, when most speakers would invite their audience to buy their book or some other lower-priced product, I instead invited my audience to go deeper with a high-ticket offer: a year-long mentorship program with a ticket price of $21K. Because it was a lot more expensive than a book, I was able to cross 6 figures in a single day.

When I told Margot that people paid me $21K to help them, she couldn't believe it. "People *do* that?" she asked.

I told her, "Yes! People do it all the time! As long as you can deliver a result that's worth it to them—about 10 times what you're charging—people will gladly pay you to get that result quickly. It doesn't matter if it's health, or relationships, or business. People love to pay mentors to help them get to the result they want, quicker. Just *think* about how much you spent on college!" I grinned.

Then I asked, "What do you help people with, Margot?"

She said, "I help people find the love of their life."

"So cool, think about how valuable that is. To finally find true love, the peace that it will bring to them, the fulfillment. Now they might even be able to plan a family! How much is that worth to someone?

"Now think about how much time they are wasting, unfulfilled, emotionally frustrated, and overwhelmed with the online dating scene. How much is that costing them?"

It was starting to sink in.

"Even if your mentorship was only $10,000. It's only 10 people at $10,000 to do a 6-figure day, and if you were in a bigger room ... 100 people at $10,000 would be all you'd need to have a 7-figure day. It happens all the time."

Margot stared at me as if I was giving her the keys to the kingdom, but unsure if she had the skill to unlock the gates.

"It's very exciting to think about," she said. "I've always wanted to offer a mastermind or mentorship program."

"It's one of the most rewarding programs I've ever offered," I told her. "I adore my clients. I really love spending time with them." I could see her mind dreaming up ideas of exotic locations and luxurious hotels for hosting events.

I could tell Margot's wheels were turning with all the possibilities.

Understand that people buy from those they feel like they know, like, and trust. As a transformational speaker, you have an opportunity to build trust through your event and offer something super valuable at the end.

Create Wealth with Your Own Event

If your wheels are turning, and you want to know more about hosting your own event, Joe and I have put together a short video training for you that you can access by going to:

MDSbonuses.com

Want to hear something else exciting?

The easiest way on the planet to host an event is to make it a virtual event!

Since March of 2020, because of the pandemic, *virtual* events have been exploding. It's never been easier. It's never been less expensive. It's never been more accessible. And 99% of the world has no *idea* it exists as a possibility. But you do because you're reading this book!

Can you imagine hosting an online group for a period of time, having amazing collaboration, teaching on a topic you love—*and* doing 6 figures in one day?

Let's have some fun:

How much would *you* like to make in the next 90–120 days? Write down that number.

How many paying clients would it take to hit that number? Now write down that number.

Pretend your closing rate at your event is 20%.

How many people need to be in the room for you to hit that number? Write that number.

If you want to make $100,000 in 90 days …

Ten ideal clients at $10,000 each …

50 people need to be at your event to get a 20% close rate with ten sales.

Could you find 50 people who would love to learn more about your specialty?

Learning how to create a transformational event is the secret to having a 6- or 7-figure "cash infusion" while changing lives. Having your own virtual event will enable you to go into enough detail so they will understand that you are a master at what you teach. In addition, your audience will develop the "know, like, and trust" factor with you so that when you make an offer, they're going to say, "This is awesome," and take you up on that offer.

Here's the bottom line:

A high-ticket offer sold at a virtual event is the fastest way to income and impact.

There isn't a more elegant method to change people's lives and the lives of your family than virtual events. They accelerate your business revenue like nothing else.

SECTION III
Closing Words

"The one easy way to become 50% more than you are now—at least—is to hone your communication skills—both written and verbal."

—Warren Buffet

19

PUTTING IT ALL TOGETHER: HOW MILLION DOLLAR SPEAKERS MOVE THEIR AUDIENCES TO SAY YES

> "Speaking is wrestling with unreasonable minds to bring them to one cohesive thought, this must be skillfully done."
>
> —T.D. Jakes

It's time for us to pass you the microphone.

The stage is yours!

With practice and mastery, you'll be able to use the skill of speaking to change your life and even the lives of your entire family for generations to come.

You have learned a lot in this book.

You learned to choose exactly who you want to serve.

You learned to listen so the audience will tell you what to talk about and even what they believe before you ever stand on the stage.

You learned that mediocre speakers focus on information, but the greats focus on transformation.

Transformation happens when you shift the thinking and beliefs with epiphanies. You ensure that newfound information becomes woven into an aspirational identity that they choose to be and declare to the world.

This all happens when the audience FEELS like buying in …

This all happens using a proven framework we discovered being used by the world's most effective speakers.

When you use the Belief and Identity Transformation System, your audience will FEEL it. This system allows you to make offers in alignment with your audience's newfound identity. It encourages you to create desire in your presentation. And it gives you the confidence to serve your audience at the deepest level.

Help them feel it by listening, creating your content and stories with speaker bits, and inviting them to their next step with a strong declaration.

Just today, I was watching a reel on Instagram, and in 60 seconds, the person on stage had the audience going crazy. The room was electric.

Guess what framework the speaker's 60-second Speaker Bit followed?

I struggle ➢ You struggle ➢ Point ➢ They say ➢ Soundbite ➢ Declaration

I heard the declarations happening and could feel the transformational power in that one-minute clip. This framework will amplify your message and unleash your audience like nothing else.

What's *your* message? Are you ready to be a Million Dollar Speaker? You have the keys. Now it's time to …

Take the stage, change some lives, and make your dreams come true.

20

YOU NEED A "FACE-SMOOSHING" DAY OF DECISION

"We're not going homeless again."

—*Joe's Wife, Saint Melody*

Hot tears rolled down my cheeks. I couldn't face her. As my frightened mind grasped for answers, I clasped my hands together, my grip getting tighter and tighter. I was afraid of what was being asked of me, but I was also afraid that I might lose her forever.

That's when my wife knelt down to take my face in her hands. She smooshed my cheeks together and looked into my eyes. She said, "I love you, honey, but I need you to make a decision. Everybody you help—their business explodes. I need you to do that for us. I need you to come through for me.

"Baby, I need you to hear me. I can't go homeless again. I just can't. I can't do it again. I know you can do it. I believe in you, but I need you to make a decision. Please, I don't care what you decide. I don't care who you decide to help. I don't care what result you try to help them to get. Really. But here's the deal, we are not going homeless again."

I couldn't breathe through my nose from all the crying, so I sat there with my lips open, feeling the air sucking through my mouth as she continued to smoosh my face. She never dropped her gaze.

"Just decide," she said. "And whatever you decide, I don't care what it is. I totally trust you to make the right decision. But whatever decision you decide on, you're going to do it for six months, period. There is no debate. There is no negotiating. There is no third option. You must do whatever you decide to do for at least six months.

"And I will give you today to decide, but we are deciding, because I'm done. I need you to hear me, baby. I need you to come through for me. I'm done. We've got to make this work, and we've got to make it work right now."

I wiped the tears from my eyes and looked off into the distance, taking in the beautiful pool and palm trees and the new environment that we had created after years of spending our life chasing the dream of changing the world. I was worried we were going to lose it all.

We had launched a nonprofit student movement and put in all of our effort to help students. We wanted to help them escape the pain of drug abuse, suicide attempts, depression, alcohol abuse, and all the other myriad issues that students go through.

We believed that if we could capture students' attention to make a difference in the world before they got caught up in all the vices and trappings of typical North American student culture, those students, inspired and empowered, would gather together as movements and change the direction of students' lives everywhere. Thereby, they would change the direction of the world.

And for a few years, our vision really exploded. But the problem was the bigger the dream, the bigger the impact; the more students that became a part of it, the more it cost us. And we were the only ones funding the vision. And so, as the vision got bigger and as the impact got bigger, the cost became bigger. And we kept investing and investing until we ran out of money.

Multiple times throughout this process, we repeated the cycle. I would go and help somebody do something, get results, make money, come back, and we'd put it all into the movement, again and again and again. Until finally, we had exhausted ourselves. We gave up on our vision. We jumped into the car and moved to Florida. And this is where you find us in the story.

The funny thing is, when I look back on my time in the nonprofit, looking for ways to fund the vision and make a difference, I repeated the same cycle over and over again. I would look for an opportunity that would be valuable and make me money.

Sitting downstairs in the basement of one of the houses that we rented for a short time (before we ran out of money for that one as well), I would start investigating. I'd look at the numbers and I'd analyze them. I remember drawing everything out on a whiteboard and getting a great idea, listening to a webinar, and deciding, "Hey, this is the thing I'm going to do."

With excitement, joy, vision, and everything that most entrepreneurs have, I would go upstairs to my wife and say, "Hey, I got it. This is the thing. This is what's going to solve it for us. This is going to get us to where we need to be."

As she listened to yet another vision of how to solve our financial situation, she would nod her head and smile. With faith and love in her eyes, she would say, "That's good. That's good. Oh my gosh. It's so cool. That's going to be awesome."

Before long, though, I would run into a roadblock. I wouldn't know how to solve the roadblock to do the thing that I had been so inspired to do from whatever webinar or training that I had recently watched.

So I would start looking around for a solution to my newfound problem. As soon as I started looking for a solution, other opportunities would come up. And I would think, *Maybe that's even better than this because then I won't have to do that and I won't have to deal with this issue. I'll do that instead.*

Then I would find yet another new opportunity. I would watch their webinar, and I'd go deep into that until I realized it was even better. And so then I would stop the thing that I was trying to do because I had hit an obstacle, and I would go find the next opportunity.

I'd tell my wife how amazing this next new opportunity was. I would describe how this was better than the other thing because of these reasons. This time, I was going to move forward. True to form, she'd nod approval and say, "Okay, babe. Yeah. I see it. That's really cool. Okay. What's next?"

So I'd start doing the next thing. And, of course, I'd hit an obstacle.

One day, I counted up the amount of time I had wasted before my wife finally did what I call the "face smoosh"—the day when she looked me in the eyes and said, "I need you to make a decision."

I did the math to see how much time actually transpired for me to decide what it was I wanted to do, who I wanted to help, who I wanted to serve, what end result I wanted to get for them.

When I did the math, I was shocked. Horrified is a better word. I was *horrified* because I realized that I had been dancing from possibility to possibility without making a decision for seven years. That's right. *Seven years.*

The more I talk to entrepreneurs, and the more I talk to leaders, the more I realize that decisions—or better yet, the lack of decisions—is the plague that destroys most dreams, most visions, and most movements.

But what distinguishes Million Dollar Speakers from mediocre ones is that they make decisions, and they make decisions quickly.

At its essence, speaking is leadership. And leaders must make decisions first to lead the people to the promised land. You have a decision to make ...

Are you going to read about it or are you going to BE IT?

Now is the time.

If you're ready to enter the world of becoming a Million Dollar Speaker so that you can use these strategies to make a difference on your platforms, join us at one of our online or in-person events where we go in-depth about everything we've talked about in this book.

To find out more about the Million Dollar Speaker Training, head over to:

MDSbonuses.com

We obviously can't do events like these forever, so if you have a burning desire to know more, be more, and do more, then in "Saint Melody's" infinite wisdom (proven effective in my life) … DECIDE QUICKLY. This is one decision that can change everything for you.

We'll see you on the stage!

SPEAK TO US

If you'd like some help using the speaking strategies in this book to grow your business, you are invited to talk to our team directly.

Just go to:

MDSspeak.com

On that page will be an application with a few questions that we need you to answer before we hop on a Zoom.

Once you complete the application, a calendar link will appear. Pick the best date and time of the available options and our team will review your answers in the application and speak with you in detail at the selected time.

The purpose of this call is to clarify your goals and see if we can help. If it's a good fit, we will discuss the options for working together. This call is primarily for people who are looking to get results quickly using the power of the stage to grow their business in a significant way.

Go to MDSspeak.com to book your call today.

ACKNOWLEDGMENTS

When you write a book, it owns a part of your heart and soul. But as creators, you can't give it your all without a team of exceptional individuals. People who will help pull you along when you want to give up, push you from behind when you're scared to forge ahead, and then walk alongside you through the good and the bad.

This book would not be possible without our families.

I, Eileen, want to thank my husband, Harrison, for being my greatest supporter. I want to thank my daughter Audrey, my son Harry, and my youngest son Oliver, for being my greatest sources of inspiration and fun. Traveling the world with you is my "why."

I, Eileen, also want to thank Myron Golden for mentoring me during a difficult season of transition for our family. What you taught us changed the game, forever. Words will never be able to describe the impact you've had on me, my children, and my clients' lives. I'm your biggest fan! Thank you.

I, Joe, want to thank my wife, Melody, who has endured the most difficult of seasons to live an adventure with me chasing God's vision in an unconventional way. Your loyalty and bravery are an inspiration to all who know our story. I'm blessed to do life with you. Thanks to both Melody and Emily for their constant reading and feedback on the many renditions of this book.

Also, thank you to Mia for project managing everything for this book and keeping everything on track.

Thank you to my many mentors, coaches, and leaders who have invested in my personal growth as a Million Dollar Speaker. Special thanks to my business coaches and mentors including James Klobasa, Myron Golden, Roland Frasier, Taylor Welch, and Russell Brunson.

Shout out to Annie Grace and Bari Baumgardner for helping come up with the name for our System: Belief and Identity Transformation System! Your insights are invaluable and it's such a privilege to be a part of Russell Brunson's Category Group Kings with you and so many other generous entrepreneurs.

We want to thank Russell Brunson, not only for writing the foreword to this book, but also for being a mentor to us during some of the most challenging times in our lives. Your coaching changed the trajectory of absolutely everything. On behalf of both our families—thank you, Russell, for your strength, for your example, and for being the greatest marketer of our generation.

We want to thank Lori Lynn for her book editing genius. Working with you and your team (eagle-eyed editing ninjas Clare Fernández, Shelby Rawson, Mary Rembert, and Jessica Welch) has been magical. Lori, you are the Fairy Godmother of Books, bringing any manuscript into harmony. You have taken all the pieces and helped us create a book that we know will help people take their messages and translate them into millions!

Special thanks also to Shanda Trofe of Transcendent Publishing for helping us nail down the title, creating the cover design, and laying out the interior for print. Your work is exceptional.

Our Elite Speakers Team, you are the hands and feet that keep things moving. Josh, Eric, Mia, Pepe, and Kara, you keep our heads pointed in the right direction and are the team that dots the "i's" and crosses the "t's." Your "no quit" attitude enables us to make Elite Speakers™ a booming enterprise that helps and serves others.

Our hope is that your life will be enriched with the knowledge that you have all the God-given tools you need to create something powerful that can impact many people. We hope we've helped to unlock that potential and launch you into the orbit of exponential success and growth!

ABOUT THE Authors

Through faith we understand that the worlds were framed by the word of God, so that things which are seen were not made of things which do appear (Heb. 11:3 KJV).

"Words are powerful."

— *Joe & Eileen*

Joseph Aaron

Joseph Aaron experienced homelessness multiple times as he worked to lead a nonprofit student movement. Now he's a go-to leader in the speaking space. Joe helps influencers, entrepreneurs, media channels, software companies, and more to create world-class events that generate 6- and even 7-figure days using the power of speaking.

Joe is a bestselling author and the co-founder of Elite Speakers, along with Eileen Wilder. He has shared the stage with some of the top industry leaders in the world today, including Les Brown, Russell Brunson, Kevin Harrington, and many more. Joe and his companies are on a mission to change the world by Multiplying Movements that Matter.

Eileen Wilder

Described as "The Queen of Stages" by major industry leaders, Eileen Wilder is the co-founder of Elite Speakers, a bestselling author, and host of the podcast, *The Confident Closer*.

She served as a pastor for over two decades, and she and her family were used to living on very humble means. That all changed one day when she found a way to make *more in a day* than she was used to making *in an entire year!*

Despite the fact that she used to be deathly afraid of public speaking, she is now one of the highest-paid speakers on the planet, having spoken on stages with Russell Brunson, Tony Robbins, and Dan Kennedy.

Her mantra?

"Do it NOW!"

WHERE TO GET YOUR

Bonuses

All the bonuses are available here:

MDSbonuses.com

This is a book on speaking. Everything you're learning to implement, you can hear and understand better with the nuance of the spoken word. For this reason, we've put together some training videos and worksheets to help you rock the stage on your next social media post or stage presentation.

If this book was helpful to you, you can go deeper in the online bonus area, where we will host the most up-to-date strategies being used to help you become a Million Dollar Speaker.

In the online bonus area, you'll find:

- speaker bits worksheets to help you prepare your next piece of content or speech
- exercises to help you make important decisions about your invitations
- examples of content that follow the speaker bits framework
- play-by-play breakdowns of the world's most effective speeches
- invitation examples
- advanced bit barrage framework examples

... and more.